Contents

Introduction

WHEN Francis Ford Coppola was preparing to film *The Godfather* he invited the principal actors to a traditional Italian dinner at his home. As Coppola remembers it, the evening developed into a sort of group improvisation with each actor behaving in the manner of the role he would play in the forthcoming film. James Caan was funny and extrovert, Robert Duvall was sociable but somehow apart from the others, while Al Pacino remained sullen and withdrawn in an effort to attract the attention of the man at the head of the table, who was accorded the respect and deference due to the patriarch he was about to portray. That man was Marlon Brando.

Brando's position as an icon of post-war cinema is virtually unassailable and, as the Coppola story illustrates, he has become something of a touchstone for younger actors. But his long-established elevation to mythic status can make it difficult to assess his actual achievement. From his earliest stage appearances, Brando was marked out by his compelling looks and the sheer physicality of his performing style. His closest contemporary rivals, James Dean and Montgomery Clift, have been equally mythologised – but only Brando has survived to older age.

Part of the secret of that survival is evident in the photographs of the young Brando as Stanley Kowalski in *A Streetcar Named Desire* or as Johnny, the leather-jacketed biker of *The Wild One*. There is little sign here of the vulnerability that was so apparent in shots of Dean and Clift at the same stage in their careers. In a sense the very power of those images has trapped Brando as a potent symbol of youthful rebellion, and as a result, he has been forbidden to grow old – with or without dignity.

Indeed, after years in the wilderness, *The Godfather* appeared to

In A Streetcar Named Desire *the open virility of Brando's appearance came as a riposte to the standard images of Hollywood stardom.*

4

mark Brando's Hollywood comeback in 1972, but the purists among his admirers gave a much warmer welcome to his performance in Bertolucci's *Last Tango In Paris* the following year. As the melancholy widower who rages over the dead body of his wife and engages in sterile sexual antics with a girl young enough to be his daughter, Brando was seen to be reviving his iconoclastic persona as a moody individualist. For all that his early performances had led critics to talk of the new dimension he brought to screen acting, he had in fact become as typecast in the public mind as Bogart, Gable and Grant had been before him.

But the restrictions of public adulation have not been the only source of disappointment in Brando's career. In many ways he has been his own worst enemy. Few actors of his stature have shown such seeming contempt for their craft. It is almost as if he is embarrassed by the memory of his youthful intensity. Some suggest he put his remarkable talent to use in attracting love and admiration to compensate for an unhappy childhood. It may also be that the praise and attention came too easily so that the grown man allowed himself the luxury of behaving like a spoilt child.

Perversely, Brando can be at his worst when playing opposite comparable talents: Trevor Howard in *Mutiny on the Bounty* and *The Saboteur*, Jack Nicholson in *The Missouri Breaks* and George C. Scott in *The Formula*. In the one film he made with his contemporary 'rival' Montgomery Clift, *The Young Lions*, it is Clift one remembers and Brando should count himself fortunate that they had no scenes together. After dropping by to watch Brando shoot a scene from that film, Clift remarked: 'Marlon is sloppy – he's using about one-tenth of his talent.'

But the talent endures. Time and again, when critics and public alike have written him off, Brando has pulled out all the stops. A trickle of indifferent, often cameo-role performances is punctuated by a characterisation of such power and clarity that the old reputation is re-established and the initial expectations are awakened once again. 'I am still here,' he seems to be saying, 'and I can still do it.'

Despite the increasingly rare glimpses of that talent, younger actors continue to emulate Brando and to point to him as the exemplar of screen acting. The veteran Hollywood star Robert Ryan once observed that Brando had 'ruined a whole generation of actors', indicating that too many young performers had modelled themselves on him to the detriment of their own individual skills. This fateful practice led Simone Signoret to express relief in her autobiography at seeing Paul Newman 'becoming Paul Newman and not just another Marlon Brando'. Much the same has been said in recent years of Robert de Niro, Al Pacino, Mickey Rourke and John Malkovich. The shadow cast by Brando is a long one.

The last great performance: Last Tango in Paris.

At the end of the Eighties, Brando ended an eight-year absence from the screen to make two films in close succession – *A Dry White Season* and *The Freshman*. His role in *A Dry White Season* is another cameo, this time as a liberal South African lawyer. The film's stand against apartheid, coupled with the fact that the director Euzhan Palcy is a young black woman, may – as some have suggested – have been the decisive factors in drawing Brando out of his 'retirement', but *The Freshman* is an outright commercial venture which casts him in a major role, a comic variant on *The Godfather's* Don Corleone. The directors of both films have praised Brando's professionalism and contribution to a happy and creative atmosphere on set. But the old contradictions were not far away. Brando celebrated his last day of shooting on *The Freshman* by denouncing the film in the Canadian press and stating categorically that he would now retire for good. This statement might have carried more weight had Brando's lawyer not been in London at that very time confirming his client's commitment to a third film – *Nostromo*.

All in all, the Marlon Brando of today seems a far cry from the dedicated and ambitious young man who would revolutionise screen technique. Those early performances in *The Men, A Streetcar Named Desire* and *On The Waterfront* remain vivid for modern audiences and, through them and a handful of more recent work, the legend persists. It is a legend that deserves close examination.

1

The making of an actor

I T MUST be admitted that the biography of a film actor is often irrelevant to an appreciation of his talent and that the revelations and insights claimed by many biographers are frequently discounted when we watch the actor at work. For example, no amount of biographical insistence that Cary Grant was a miserly wife-beater and closet homosexual can diminish the image of impeccable wit and charm that still flickers on television and repertory cinema screens throughout the world. If properly cultivated, the image is impregnable. As such, it can be a comfortingly protective barrier or, from time to time, a prison. In the case of Marlon Brando it is both.

Brando belongs to that elite group of actors – Garbo and Olivier were others – who can readily be identified by a single, image-bearing name. But while Olivier is remembered in a variety of guises, and Garbo in a variety of moods, Brando is invariably recalled as the young rebel whose total contempt for authority symbolised liberation for those who came to maturity in the immediate post-war years. Millions of young men strove to imitate Brando's negligent manner, although often, they already had something more telling in common: a shared background in America's conservative middle-class. For them, Brando epitomised the rejection of their parents' values and the birth of a generation that would pride itself on its lack of illusions. And yet, some of this generation were destined to become the bewildered parents of anti-war demonstrators while many more would find themselves bereaved by the traumatic conflict in Vietnam. By then, they would have stopped looking to Brando for guidance and, in any case, their children would have adopted the Brando image for themselves.

That the image of Brando, defiant and challenging, was kept alive during the Vietnam era was thanks in part to the thousands of wall

Marlon Brando, the dedicated and ambitious young theatre actor, photographed by Cecil Beaton in New York in 1948.

8

The two-year-old Brando at home in Omaha, Nebraska (below). Brando at six (bottom) personified the nice, middle-class American boy.

posters that hung beside images of Marilyn Monroe and Che Guevara in the bedrooms of students all over America and Europe. But Brando the actor was accounted a spent force and the man, on his rare public appearances, was considered little more than an ageing 'enfant terrible'. He was not allowed the luxury of sharing his contemporaries' disillusionment. They had not wanted him to be like them; quite the opposite: they wanted a hero. But he was not a hero, just an actor – albeit an incredibly gifted one who would soon demonstrate that his career was far from over – and he was, whether they liked it or not, very much like them.

Indeed, his childhood was typical of many middle-Americans of his generation. He was born, the third child and only son of Marlon Brando Snr. and Dorothy Pennebaker Brando, on 3rd April, 1924 in Omaha, Nebraska. The Brando line had been so long established in the American mid-west that the origin of the family name was, even then, faintly obscure. It may have been French or Dutch-Alsatian but it had already been anglicised to 'Brandow' when Marlon Snr. simplified it further to the form that his son would make famous.

On the surface, Marlon and Dorothy Brando seemed a happy and prosperous couple with a five-bedroomed house and a small domestic staff in attendance. In truth, they were somewhat ill-matched and the tensions in their relationship grew rapidly throughout their son's childhood. Much has been made of the disparity between the actor's parents in an effort to explain his rebellious behaviour in later years. There is no doubt that some unsettling events in his childhood left their mark on the man, but for the most part it is a fairly predictable story of middle class marital tension.

Brando's father made a healthy living as a sales executive for an agricultural goods company. He was known and respected in his neighbourhood and at the local Episcopal church, although his work took him away from home for long periods of time. While her husband was a pillar of local commerce, Dorothy Brando was much more concerned with the artistic life of the community. She took a keen interest in literature and was an active painter and sculptor. Her primary concern, though, was the theatre. She became a director of the Omaha Community Playhouse where she appeared with some distinction in a number of plays, including Eugene O'Neill's *Beyond the Horizon* in which she starred, in 1928, opposite a shy local boy called Henry Fonda.

The Brando children – Jocelyn, Frances and 'Bud' (as young Marlon was known at the time) – enjoyed the variety of experience engendered by their mother's cultural interests. Dorothy often played hostess to local actors, writers and artists with the result that the children were exposed to the arts from an early age. Meanwhile, their domestic stability was maintained by Marlon Senior's steady income. What the children did not know was that their father's long spells out of town had led him to pursue a series of casual affairs and that Dorothy had become increasingly dependent on alcohol to sustain herself for her demanding theatrical commitments. Her problem became even more acute when the coming of the Depression forced the family to re-locate near Chicago.

They moved to Evanston, Illinois, a town noted then and now for its firm devotion to the ideals of temperance. In fact, it is still illegal to serve alcoholic drinks there. Anyone with a drink problem was bound to have a difficult time during America's Prohibition years, but Dorothy would find it especially hard to settle with her family in a town where society generally was conditioned to disapprove of her. In addition, she had been forced to abandon the Omaha Playhouse which had become central to her life and there was no equivalent in Evanston. The strain on the Brando marriage began to show, and to be felt by the children.

From a material point of view, the Brandos did not suffer too badly in the Depression and they were able to rent a house in a fashionable district of Evanston. Young Marlon attended the local Lincoln School where he met and befriended a fellow pupil, Wally Cox. Some biographers have pointed to this friendship as an attraction of opposites in that Cox was small and frail with an interest in cerebral rather than athletic pursuits while Brando was a keen footballer and participant in track events. In fact, the two boys shared the same problem of poor eyesight and Brando, who wore a brace to correct his irregular teeth, was obsessed with his minor physical shortcomings, particularly his lack of height. In later years, and with Brando's encouragement, Cox would become a gifted comedy actor enjoying a brief period of television fame as *Mr. Peepers* and Paul Gallico's *Hiram Holliday*. The two remained close until Cox's premature death in 1972.

The Brando family remained in Evanston until 1938 when Marlon was fourteen and less easily protected from awareness of his mother's alcoholism and his father's recurrent infidelity. Predictably, the restrictive social climate of a town so rigidly opposed to alcohol had exacerbated Dorothy Brando's condition and all but forced her to move away. Dorothy went with the children to stay with her sister, Bette Lindemeyer in California until Marlon Senior was able to rent their new house – an eight-acre farm – in the more rural Illinois town of Libertyville.

If, as Cox and others have testified, Brando was a disruptive influence at Lincoln School it was not so much the behaviour of a determined rebel as an obvious reaction to the disquiet in his home life. Matters did not improve after his enrolment at Libertyville Township School. By turns boisterous and introspective, he was frequently absent from

Thirty years before One-Eyed Jacks, *young Marlon in cowboy gear (below). With his sisters Frances and Jocelyn in Evanston, Illinois (bottom).*

classes and proved a difficult student for teachers to manage. In later years, however, his Libertyville principal made a point of saying that Brando had no real meanness of spirit and was generally accounted nothing more than 'irresponsible'.

The clash of temperaments between Dorothy Brando and her husband extended, not unnaturally, to their parental attitudes. Dorothy was all for giving her children a free rein while her husband took a firmer, more restraining line, especially with his son. Having observed – and approved of – the boy's growing interest in athletics and physical culture, he resolved to send him to his own former training ground, Shattuck Military Academy in Faribult, Minnesota. Despite Dorothy's objections, Marlon was taken out of Libertyville Township (he would later claim he had been expelled) and, at the age of 17, he was packed off to Shattuck in 1941.

If this was an attempt by the father to impose some much needed discipline or even to establish a late rapport with the teenage son who had all but lost respect for him, it failed. Ironically, it served to bring Brando even closer to his mother because, although he disliked Shattuck intensely, it was here that he made his first appearance on a stage. He played the leading role of an explorer in a student production of *A Message From Khufu*, a melodrama which centred on Egyptology. This was followed by smaller roles in subsequent productions and extra-curricular studies of the works of Shakespeare.

Brando used his developing acting talent in less official ways, too, faking a variety of illnesses and even acquiring a pronounced limp to avoid the only other activity he professed to enjoy – close order drill.

As a member of Shattuck's Crack Drill Squad – which his father had joined in 1916 – Brando put in two hundred hours of arduous training for an annual public demonstration which lasted only twenty minutes. In 1943, when he dropped out of the squad by exaggerating a genuine knee injury, he was put on probation and ordered to report for daily inspection or else stay put in the school's hospital. He broke the probation by taking an unauthorised trip out of the school grounds and was summarily expelled. In this case, the expulsion was real but Brando would later 'improve' the reasons for it by saying that he had built a bomb out of firecrackers to revenge himself against an unpopular teacher. In Brando's version, the fuse for the bomb – a trail of hair tonic – failed to disappear as planned but instead left a scorch mark that led directly to his room, and so he was caught.

'The Brando Version', a romanticised re-working of key events in his early life, has been aided by a number of self-appointed (and often unreliable) Boswells who traded on their famous friend's success. Add to this the contributions of scores of press agents and gossip columnists, all intent in perpetuating the myth of the 'mixed-up kid', and it is not hard to see why the facts of Brando's biography are frequently clouded

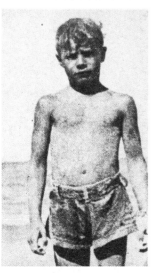

Brando was, by all accounts, an unremarkable student. His mature attempts at writing would prove ineffective (below). Marlon at ten (bottom), already manifesting the truculent stare.

from this point. Given his family circumstances, it is hardly surprising that Brando was something of a problem in his student days but a large number of his contemporaries remember the young Marlon Brando as a quiet, polite – even charming – man. During his early stage career he enjoyed playing fast and loose with the truth, claiming in some programme notes to have been born in Rangoon or Calcutta. This was such an obvious game that perhaps he barely noticed when things got out of hand, or maybe it was his way of countering early fame with an attempt to cling to some sort of private life. As the newspaper editor in John Ford's *The Man Who Shot Liberty Valance* said: 'When the legend becomes the truth, print the legend.' How much truth or legend there is in any biography of Marlon Brando is open to question.

As a corrective to the idea of Brando as the congenital outsider Nuba Fletcher – who was Shattuck's civilian headmaster in Brando's time at the Academy – has testified that his expulsion from the Academy was met with a petition from the other cadets demanding Brando's re-instatement. Fletcher decided to give the boy another chance, but Brando showed no interest in going back. He had damaged his knee in a football game, and the verdict of Hudson Mealey, one of his Shattuck team-mates, on Brando the footballer pre-figure the critical response that would be heard so often in his late acting career: '[Brando] was always horsing around. He could have been a terrific athlete. He was very fast on his feet and had a magnificent physique. But he didn't hold to his form'.

When Brando returned home from Shattuck, America was at war. He was of an age to be called up but was graded 4-F and exempted as a result of his myopia and that knee injury. One of the traits that had made Brando so popular at Shattuck was his concern for the underdog – something which had been evident throughout his childhood. Whether he was rescuing an injured animal or bird, or else taking an unfashionably belligerent stance in favour of racial equality Brando was known for his sincere and good-humoured idealism. Perhaps it was this that led him to declare a brief interest in going into the church as a minister or preacher – a kindred vocation with the theatre, but far more respectable. His family dissuaded him. His sisters Jocelyn and Frances had both moved to New York and Marlon, unwilling or unable to face life alone with his parents, chose to follow them, taking on a number of temporary jobs while he decided what to do with his life.

In New York, Jocelyn had already embarked on an acting career (in which she would soon receive encouragement from Dorothy Brando's old associate, Henry Fonda) and Frances was studying art. Marlon moved in with Frances and, after prompting from both sisters (and a promise of financial help from his father), agreed to enrol in acting classes at the New School for Social Research, a liberal arts college which emphasised experimentation over traditional academic styles and

A fourteen-year-old Brando with Jocelyn and Frances. Jocelyn's acting ambitions would spur Brando's own (below). Brando at Shattuck Military Academy (bottom).

qualifications. 'I'm often asked why I did that,' he said some years later, 'Really it was only chance. My sister Jocelyn was already acting, and I thought I'd like to give it a whirl too.' But Bette Lindemeyer recalled that when her nephew was fifteen he had gone with his mother and sisters to visit Henry Fonda on a Hollywood film set. Fonda, Mrs. Lindemeyer insisted, had a profound impact on the boy. It may have been that Brando was simply, and understandably, impressed by encountering a famous movie star face to face, but his aunt was certain that his long period of brooding after the meeting indicated his first serious consideration of the notion of a career as an actor.

The Dramatic Workshop at the New School for Social Research was run by Erwin Piscator, a refugee from Hitler's Germany and one-time protégé of Max Reinhardt. Piscator directed student productions at the School, but the classes Brando attended were taught by Stella Adler. Miss Adler had had a distinguished career in the New York theatre, beginning with the traditional Yiddish companies before moving on to Broadway. With her husband, the influential theatre critic and director Harold Clurman, she had been a founder member of the Group Theatre which had broken away from the more conservative Theatre Guild.

The Group was associated with writers such as Clifford Odets and Irwin Shaw and was famous for its agit-prop style of 'socially conscious' productions. Among those who worked in the Group's productions and found later fame in the movies were John Garfield, Franchot Tone, Lee J. Cobb and Elia Kazan – who also moved on to film directing. Kazan once summed up the Group Theatre experience as 'the most seminal event in the history of the American theatre, perhaps more because of its influence than its accomplishments'. In the brief hiatus between the demise of the Group Theatre and the founding of the Actors' Studio, Stella Adler brought the teaching techniques of Constantin Stanislavski, with whom she had studied, to the classrooms of the New School. Among the students who passed through the School in the mid-forties were Walter Matthau, Harry Belafonte, Elaine Stritch and the writers Tennessee Williams and James Baldwin.

Stella Adler was undoubtedly the first person to recognise Brando's exceptional talent. He had been in her class for only a week when she said: 'Within a year, Marlon Brando will be the best actor in the American theatre.' In later years she would describe his acting style as 'the perfect marriage of intuition and intelligence', observing modestly that she 'taught him nothing. I opened up the possibilities of thinking, feeling, experiencing, and as I opened up those doors, he walked right through'. The very naturalness of Brando's acting made for an impression of spontaneity, but it was an impression he often found hard to maintain.

When Erwin Piscator came to cast Brando in his first college production, he gave him two roles (one of them as a giraffe) in a children's play, *Bobino*. This incongruous debut was followed by more substantial parts for Brando, among them Sebastian in *Twelfth Night* and a dual role as a teacher and an angel in Gerhardt Hauptmann's *Hannele's Way to Heaven*. These last two plays, nominally directed by Piscator, were taken to Long Island for a short season in the summer of 1944. In practice, at least in the case of the Shakespeare, the direction was handled by Piscator's wife, Maria, while her husband was fulfilling a contract job on Broadway. Maria Piscator lacked the necessary fire to drill discipline into the company with the result that, as one of Brando's fellow cast members, Carlo Fiore recalled, 'We were not so much performing as reaching for our lines.' In such loosely structured conditions, Brando's irresponsibility resurfaced. He foolishly placed himself in an innocent but compromising position with one of the actresses – Piscator returned to find them asleep on the same bed – and he was dropped from the cast.

Hannele's Way to Heaven and *Twelfth Night* provided Brando with his first newspaper reviews in the New York *Morning Telegraph*. Their drama critic, George Freedley wrote that Brando was the best actor in the Hauptmann play and said of *Twelfth Night*: 'Marlon Brando handled the tiny part of Sebastian satisfactorily, though it would have been interesting to see what he might have done with Feste or Orsino.'

With Stella Adler's encouragement, Brando auditioned for his first commercial engagement in John Van Druten's *I Remember Mama*. The play was a sentimental drama about a Norwegian-American immigrant family in turn-of-the-century San Francisco, and it was produced by the musical-writing team, Rodgers and Hammerstein. Neither producer was impressed by Brando's audition (his first) which was clumsy and ill-prepared, but Van Druten felt a quality which would suit the role of Nels, the 15-year-old son of the family. The 20-year-old Brando was given the part, and the play opened successfully in October 1944 at New York's Music Box Theatre and ran for 713 performances. Only one reviewer specifically mentioned Brando: 'The Nels of Marlon Brando' said the critic of the New York *Journal-American*, 'is, if he doesn't mind my saying so, charming.' That line would certainly acquire an irony in future years.

The success of *I Remember Mama* brought Brando to the attention of Broadway's top agents, one of whom, Edith Van Cleve of MCA, managed to get him to sign up, with the interesting proviso that he was not interested in film offers. Brando continued to attend classes at the New School throughout the run of the Van Druten play, and Stella Adler retained a strong interest in his career. As the play's run came to an end, Van Cleve sent Brando to audition for Alfred Lunt and Lynne Fontanne who were presenting their London success, *Love in Idleness* on Broadway under the title, *O Mistress Mine*. Lunt and Fontanne

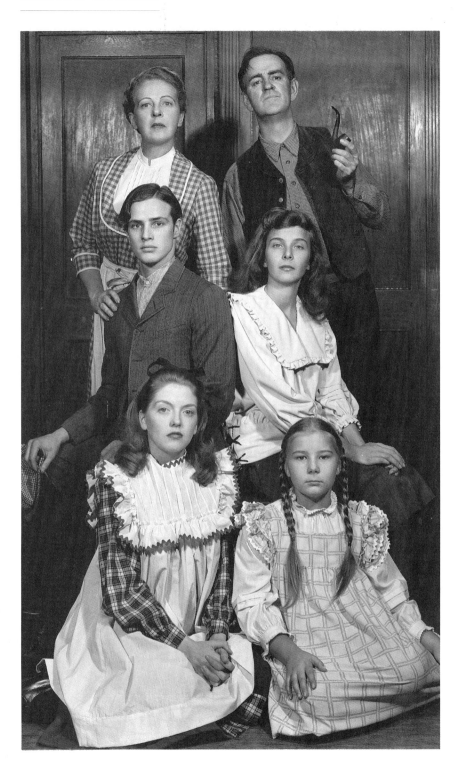

Brando (middle row, left) reached Broadway in 1944 in the successful John Van Druten play I Remember Mama, *a sentimental evocation of Norwegian-American life at the turn of the century.*

were Broadway's most celebrated acting partnership, but their style – and that of the play's author, Terence Rattigan – was a long way from the kind of thing Brando had been striving for in his classes with Miss Adler. In any event, he gave a poor reading and the Lunts considered him too old for the part in question. It is part of the Brando legend that he did not read for the Lunts at all but mumbled the nursery rhyme, 'Hickory, dickory, dock', before strolling off the stage. When Lunt was told this story, some years later, he remarked, 'I imagine that when he became famous, Brando decided to make a character for himself, and rudeness was part of that character.'

Once again, it was Stella Adler who would provide a suitable showcase for Brando. In 1946, Adler's husband Harold Clurman teamed up with his Group Theatre colleague Elia Kazan to present Maxwell Anderson's *Truckline Cafe* and found himself being persuaded to give his wife's young pupil a small role. Elia Kazan recently admitted that he has all but forgotten this particular play 'except for one thing. It had a five-minute scene with a young man who completely dominated the stage and the audience with an overwhelming emotional power that is now, in my memory, and then, on stage, unforgettable. The young man's name was Marlon Brando.'

Anderson's play was set in a roadside diner patronised by a variety of characters, each one coming to terms with the uncertainty of the post-war future. The New York critics were unanimous in their dislike of the play, citing Anderson's tendency to locate the true drama offstage, leaving the actors burdened by ponderous, expository dialogue. Brando's character was Sage McRae, a combat veteran who murders his faithless wife, becomes a fugitive and finally pours out his story to a waitress before giving himself up to the police. The complexities of this character had to be conveyed in two brief scenes (neither of which showed the actual murder). Carlo Fiore, Brando's colleague from the Piscator season, described his shock at seeing Brando's appearance in the first of these scenes. As the battle-fatigued McRae, Fiore said 'Brando looked emaciated. Of course his debilitated appearance did enhance the characterisation,' Fiore continued, 'but endangering one's health to give verisimilitude to a performance was carrying an actor's responsibility to his role too far.'

In fact, Brando's health was in no real danger but he had been put through a gruelling rehearsal schedule by Harold Clurman who was keen to curb the actor's tendency to under-project his voice. Clurman's unorthodox technique involved placing Brando alone on stage and forcing him to scream loudly. To prepare the actor for the difficult second scene in which McRae re-enters the deserted diner after the murder and also after his own failed attempt to drown himself in the nearby lake, Clurman had two stagehands drench Brando in freezing cold water moments before his entrance.

With Ann Shepherd in Maxwell Anderson's short-lived Truckline Cafe. *Brando played the returning combat veteran Sage McRae in a play which reflected post-war uncertainty.*

17

In I Remember Mama *Brando (here with Richard Bishop and Mady Christians) gives his first portrayal of rebellious youth. The only reviewer to mention him considered him 'charming'.*

Truckline Cafe was not a good play and the production was far from Clurman's best work, but its significance in the development of Brando as an actor should not be underestimated. His performance did not save the show from early closure, but his final exit into the arms of the waiting posse regularly earned him a standing ovation and the plaudits of important critics such as Burton Rascoe and George Jean Nathan. In his Review of 1946, Nathan wrote that Brando gave 'one of the especially interesting performances of the season'.

The director Jules Dassin recalled watching Brando in the Anderson play and thinking 'Oh, shit, this kid is great', and another witness was the future film critic, Pauline Kael. In her essay on *Last Tango in Paris*, Kael remembered arriving late for a performance of *Truckline Cafe* '...I looked up and saw what I thought was an actor having a seizure on stage. Embarrassed for him, I lowered my eyes, and it wasn't until the young man who'd brought me grabbed my arm and said, "Watch this guy!" that I realised that he was acting. I think a lot of people will make my old mistake when they see Brando's performance as Paul [in *Last Tango*]. I think some may prefer to make this mistake, so they won't have to recognise how deep down he goes and what he dredges up.' *Truckline Cafe* did not make Brando a star, but it established his reputation as an actor of remarkable talent and led him, within a year, to his greatest stage role.

Larger roles followed in the ensuing months, but none of them allowed him the chance to match his portrayal of Sage McRae. In New York he followed in the footsteps of Orson Welles and Burgess Meredith in playing the difficult role of Marchbanks, the fey young poet, in a Broadway revival of Bernard Shaw's *Candida* opposite Katherine Cornell, then a major star of American theatre who made a speciality of this particular play. The production was, as usual, directed by Cornell's husband, Guthrie McClintic but the show – which had a short run – was little more than a 'filler', occupying the matinee slots that had come vacant because of the poor reception for McClintic's production of Anouilh's *Antigone*.

Cornell's co-star was Sir Cedric Hardwicke who – in his autobiography, *A Victorian in Orbit* – declared Brando 'useless' as Marchbanks, although he admitted to detecting talent in him. Cornell herself was more generous, saying that 'at the top of his form [Brando] was the finest Marchbanks I ever had'. The contradictions did not stop with his performance: on a personal level, Hardwicke thought Brando 'appallingly rude' while Cornell said he was 'warm and friendly and interesting'.

The Shavian disappointment was closely followed by an even more curious venture, *A Flag is Born* by Ben Hecht (who co-wrote the classic newspaper comedy, *The Front Page*). This play, with music by Kurt Weill, starred Paul Muni and was directed by Stella Adler's brother,

Brando's role in Truckline Cafe *(here with Ann Shepherd) was small but intensely dramatic, allowing him to take his first steps towards the technique which would invigorate American acting.*

19

the actor-director Luther Adler. Written in the form of a pageant, the play was designed to promote the notion of a Jewish state in Palestine and Hecht did nothing to disguise his commitment to the often violent tactics of the Irgun freedom fighters. Soon afterwards, he would take out a newspaper advertisement in which he announced that every time a British soldier died 'I have a little holiday in my heart'. This would be too much for many of Hecht's supporters (including Brando) who would distance themselves from the writer in future years. Brando's performance in *A Flag is Born* drew respectable notices, but the play itself was not well received.

After *A Flag is Born*, Brando joined Tallulah Bankhead in the try-out run of Jean Cocteau's *The Eagle Has Two Heads* which had been a great success in Paris and London. It was not however to American tastes and the director, John C. Wilson was ill-equipped to cope with the overbearing Miss Bankhead. Brando and Bankhead did not work well together. He reportedly became so incensed by her self-centred behaviour that he frequently up-staged her by inventing 'business' for himself during her big speeches. It is also suggested that he strongly resisted her predatory sexual advances. Whatever the truth of the matter, Brando was replaced by Helmut Dantine before the play reached Broadway. Among those who saw the Cocteau play during the Newhaven try-out while Brando was still in the cast was another gifted young actor, Montgomery Clift. In fact, Clift had been asked to take over the role for the Broadway run but he turned it down. Having already seen and been greatly impressed by Brando's performance in *Truckline Cafe,* Clift was interested to see the man who was already being touted as his rival in a different role. They met on the train back to New York that night and, after an initial guardedness, got along together amicably by avoiding all mention of the play.

Back in New York, Brando was reunited with his old schoolfriend Wally Cox who was supporting himself and his invalid mother by making costume jewellery. Cox lived in a rundown apartment in a 10th Street tenement block, but Brando found the atmosphere there appealing and spent a great deal of time in extended visits, often bringing one of his many girlfriends with him. Although the two men had not seen each other for several years – and their physical differences were now more pronounced then ever – theirs was a very close friendship.

Freed from theatrical commitments, Brando attended classes with Robert Lewis and Elia Kazan at the newly-formed Actors' Studio and asked Edith Van Cleve to scout a film script for him. His last three productions having been less than happy experiences, Brando was concerned in case he acquired a reputation for being difficult. He even tried his hand at directing at the Studio, with Julie Harris in an Americanised version of Ibsen's *Hedda Gabler*.

As a young actor Brando worked hard to keep himself in good physical shape.

Despite the fact that his career was building respectably, Brando was not yet a star and that limited the options that Van Cleve could obtain from the major film studios, as Brando didn't want to be saddled with a long term contract. A chance presented itself when Elia Kazan, who had begun a parallel career as a film director, had been invited to direct a 'social conscience' picture for Twentieth-Century Fox. The film was *Gentleman's Agreement* with a script by Moss Hart that professed to be an outspoken attack on anti-semitism. Gregory Peck had already been cast as a writer – a gentile – who poses as a Jew to study the nature of prejudice. There was a secondary role, that of a real Jew, which Kazan had offered to his old associate, John Garfield, who was undecided. For a while, Kazan considered Brando for the role, but when Garfield finally agreed the idea was dropped.

Garfield had been a fine stage actor whose rugged looks had brought him great success in Hollywood. What had worried him about *Gentleman's Agreement* was the drop in status that would come if he accepted a supporting role in a film whose 'risky' subject matter might impair its success. When the film was finished, Kazan approached Garfield again – this time to play a leading role in the theatre. Once again Garfield hesitated. As it happened, *Gentleman's Agreement* did provide his screen career with just the impetus it needed – it seemed foolish to move back to New York and take a chance on an untried play. He felt too that the character he was being offered was 'underwritten' – the play quite clearly centred on the female character lead. This time Kazan did not wait for Garfield to come round to the idea. After briefly considering Burt Lancaster, whose agent made too many excessive demands, Kazan asked Brando to look at the part. Brando was reluctant to say yes, but not for the same reason as Garfield. He recognised the power of the writing and could see that the role would be a challenge but the character was so removed from his own attitudes and life experience that he feared he would not be able to manage it. The play in question was, of course, *A Streetcar Named Desire* and the role – which would forever be associated with Marlon Brando – was that of Stanley Kowalski.

Overriding Brando's objections, Kazan lent him the money to travel to Provincetown where he could meet the playwright Tennessee Williams. Williams waited two days for the young actor's arrival – Brando had needed the money to eat and had decided to hitch to the coast. When he finally showed up he found Williams worrying about the condition of his house's plumbing and electricity supply. Before sitting down to read the play Brando took both of these practical matters in hand then proceeded, in Williams' words, to 'read the script aloud, just as he played it. It was the most magnificent reading I ever heard and he had the part immediately. He stayed the night, curled up on the floor.'

The disconcerting 'moodiness' of the young Brando (above) would soon be adopted by such contemporaries as James Dean and Paul Newman. In 1948, Brando looked set for a brilliant stage career, but within a year of this Cecil Beaton photo session (right), he would have abandoned the theatre for Hollywood.

2

The birth
of a star

I T IS hard to appreciate the considerable impact of the first production of *A Streetcar Named Desire* now that the play has acquired its status as a modern classic. But in 1947 the intensely charged relationship between Stanley Kowalski and his sister-in-law Blanche du Bois shocked and disturbed the Broadway audience. In particular, the open sexuality of Brando's performance drew the attention of critics and public alike to such a degree that Kazan feared that the play might be thrown out of balance or reduced to 'a moral fable of the brutalisation of a sensitive soul by a sadistic bully'. Confiding his fears to Tennessee Williams, Kazan found the playwright totally unconcerned by the problem and concluded that he was 'riding a crush' on the young actor. After his visit to Tennessee Williams Brando had joined the rest of the cast of *Streetcar* – Jessica Tandy as Blanche, Kim Hunter as Stella and Karl Malden as Mitch – for rehearsals in New York. The rehearsal period was difficult, but only from the demands of the play. All the participants have recalled it as a happy time, secure in the knowledge that they were working on a piece of great quality. Kazan worked hard with Brando, convincing him that the role was more than a case of Sage McRae writ large.

For Jessica Tandy, English-born and classically trained, Brando's approach placed great demands on her resources. She had had to fight hard to get the role of Blanche as neither Kazan nor the play's producer Irene Mayer Selznick had wanted an English actress for the part. Tandy had gone so far as to mount a 'showcase audition' when, under the direction of her husband Hume Cronyn, she appeared in a production of *Portrait of a Madonna*, an earlier Williams play which formed the basis for *Streetcar*. Throughout the rehearsal period and on into the first provincial try-outs, Kazan and Tandy worked closely to

Brando's off-stage appearance was casual but nothing like the 'slob' image which would be projected by the gossip columnists.

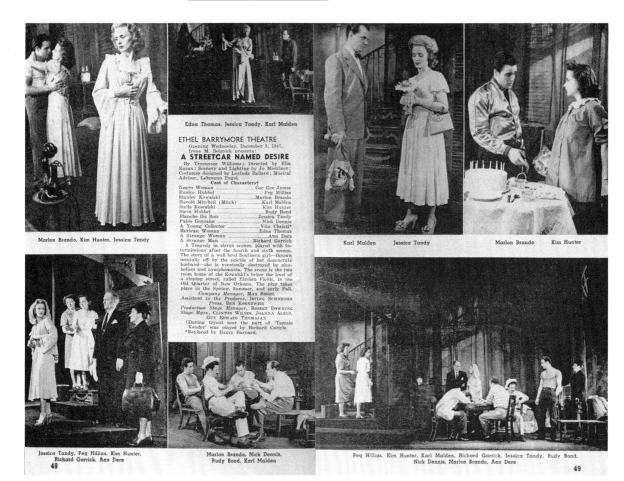

Marlon Brando, Kim Hunter, Jessica Tandy

Edna Thomas, Jessica Tandy, Karl Malden

ETHEL BARRYMORE THEATRE

Opening Wednesday, December 3, 1947.
Irene M. Selznick presents:

A STREETCAR NAMED DESIRE

By Tennessee Williams; Directed by Elia
Kazan; Scenery and Lighting by Jo Mielziner;
Costumes designed by Lucinda Ballard; Musical
Advisor, Lehmann Engel.

Cast of Characters†

Negro Woman _____ Gee Gee James
Eunice Hubbel _____ Peg Hillias
Stanley Kowalski _____ Marlon Brando
Harold Mitchell (Mitch) _____ Karl Malden
Stella Kowalski _____ Kim Hunter
Steve Hubbel _____ Rudy Bond
Blanche Du Bois _____ Jessica Tandy
Pablo Gonzales _____ Nick Dennis
A Young Collector _____ Vito Christi*
Mexican Woman _____ Edna Thomas
A Strange Woman _____ Ann Dere
A Strange Man _____ Richard Garrick

A Tragedy in eleven scenes, played with in-
termissions after the fourth and sixth scenes.
The story of a well bred Southern girl—thrown
mentally off by the suicide of her degenerate
husband—she is eventually destroyed by alcoholism and nymphomania. The scene is the two
room home of the Kowalski's below the level of
a sloping street, called Elysian Fields, in the
Old Quarter of New Orleans. The play takes
place in the Spring, Summer, and early Fall.

Company Manager, MAX SIEGEL.
Assistant to the Producer, IRVING SCHNEIDER
Press, BEN KORNZWEIG
Production Stage Manager, ROBERT DOWNING
Stage Mgrs., CLINTON WILDER, JOANNA ALBUS,
GUY EDWARD THOMAJAN

†During tryout tour the part of 'Tamale
Vendor' was played by Richard Carlyle.
*Replaced by Henry Barnard.

Karl Malden   Jessica Tandy

Marlon Brando   Kim Hunter

Jessica Tandy, Peg Hillias, Kim Hunter,
Richard Garrick, Ann Dere
48

Marlon Brando, Nick Dennis,
Rudy Bond, Karl Malden

Peg Hillias, Kim Hunter, Karl Malden, Richard Garrick, Jessica Tandy, Rudy Bond,
Nick Dennis, Marlon Brando, Ann Dere
49

This spread in Theatre World *magazine heralded the Broadway opening of* A Streetcar Named Desire. *Brando, Kim Hunter and Karl Malden would go on to repeat their roles in Kazan's film version, but Jessica Tandy as Blanche would be replaced by the more 'bankable' Vivien Leigh.*

establish Blanche in the face of Brando's extraordinary incarnation of Stanley. Just how difficult this could be was indicated by Kim Hunter who played Stella, Stanley's wife and Blanche's sister, and who recalled Brando's habit of changing line emphases and physical actions not only during the rehearsal period but throughout the run of the play. Hunter found this exhilarating and praised Brando's 'uncanny sense of truth' adding that 'he yanks you into his own sense of reality' but, as a graduate of the Actors Studio, she might be expected more readily than Tandy to appreciate Brando's 'freestyle' methods. Ultimately, as is often the case when major talents from different disciplines work together, it was a question of Tandy and Brando getting the measure of each other. It has often been suggested that Tandy disapproved of Brando, both personally and professionally but as Kazan makes clear in his autobiography: 'Jessie was show-smart; she knew that actors give better performances when they work with partners whose talents challenge their own.'

By the time *Streetcar* opened at the Ethel Barrymore Theatre, New York on 3rd December, 1947, the cast were secure in their roles and the unanimously favourable reviews guaranteed the play's success. The judgements of the critics confirmed Kazan's and Williams' belief in their leading man. As an established star Jessica Tandy received the best reviews but critic after critic hailed Brando's performance as 'brilliant' (*PM*), 'magnificent' (*New York Daily News*), while the New York *Journal-American* praised 'our theatre's most memorable young actor at his most memorable'. The Drama Critics Circle voted *Streetcar*

Brando's performance as Stanley Kowalski in the stage production of Streetcar *(here with Jessica Tandy as Blanche) established the 23-year-old actor as a major star.*

best play of the year, confirming Tennessee Williams' reputation and winning him the Pulitzer Prize, and it made Brando a star. It was the peak of his short theatrical career, and while he could hardly have been aware of it, it was also the virtual end of it. He would appear on stage again, but only briefly and with indifferent results. Even as the New York theatre was acclaiming its brightest hope it was about to lose him. From now on he would give the best of himself to a medium he had affected to scorn, the cinema – and he would alter the face of American screen acting for ever.

Brando was now a celebrity, the subject of newspaper interviews and magazine profiles (although he shared the spotlight with his sisters in 'The Brandos', a 1948 feature in *Life* magazine). Brando responded playfully to this sudden rush of attention, taking the opportunity to add to his fanciful descriptions of himself. He may have been naive, but he was matched here by the credulity of the journalists who lent a solemn authority to scores of facetious remarks.

There is no doubt that the necessary repetition of a long theatrical run bored Brando. Tandy, Hunter and Malden were able to absorb his constant changes of pace and attack but it cannot have escaped their notice that this unusual technique was inclined to give Brando the leading edge in performance. Some observers may have found this exciting but it may just as easily be construed as unprofessional behaviour. For all his freshness and brilliance, he was practising a very effective form of one-upmanship. Time after time, Brando has denigrated acting as a craft and laughed engagingly when he has been dubbed the 'greatest' of American actors. But, as his behaviour in *Streetcar* demonstrated, he has often taken a fiercely competitive approach to his work.

The role of Stanley Kowalski was a demanding one, but it allowed Brando a twenty-minute period off-stage each night. Eager to keep himself fully occupied rather than allow his performance to cool down, Brando took to sparring with his understudy Jack Palance – an accomplished boxer – and with other members of the cast. One night, he had a short bout with Nick Dennis who was playing one of Kowalski's poker-night cronies in the play. Dennis slipped easily under Brando's guard and delivered a punch which flattened the star's nose. Staunching the blood with a handkerchief, Brando went on and finished the play – much to the alarm of Jessica Tandy and the rest of the cast. When the show was over he was taken to a hospital where it was discovered that his nose was broken. When Irene Selznick came to visit her injured star, Brando had his face made up to make his injuries appear much worse – then he lay in bed and feigned agony. Shocked, Selznick immediately gave him a two-week holiday. Forty years after the incident, Brando was still regaling interviewers with the story of this little joke. It was to be an expensive prank in terms of the nose itself, which was unable to set properly because of Brando's constant re-arrangement of the bandages for dramatic effect. But Brando was quick to accept his altered physiognomy, believing that it added a measure of virility that had earlier been missing. Irene Selznick felt the same way, observing much later of Brando's accident: 'Before it, he was just too beautiful.'

Brando stayed with *Streetcar* for eighteen months, growing ever more restless day by day. When he began to depart from the written text, Selznick sent for Tennessee Williams in an effort to bring the actor into line. Williams was unconcerned by Brando's variations and said: 'Let him play it his way, it's better.' Off-stage, Brando expressed contempt for those who seemed to expect him to be Kowalski in his everyday life. 'Kowalski was always right and never afraid,' he would later remark. 'He never doubted himself. His ego was very secure and he had the kind of brutal aggressiveness I hate. I'm afraid of it. I detest the character.' If we are to take Brando at his word, it can be assumed that he was masking his private fear and insecurity beneath the vulgar clowning and the apparent arrogance that marked his attitude to performance. That Brando was not the egocentric oddball portrayed in contemporary accounts is attested by Karl Malden's recollection of working with him on *Streetcar*. Malden, playing the mother-dominated Mitch who provides a brief romatic interlude for Blanche, found that the ever-changing Brando would frequently catch him off-guard and cause him difficulties with his own performance. Taking Brando to one side, Malden explained the problem and discovered Brando to be a model of consideration and flexibility. He seemed to Malden to be genuinely concerned with the life of the piece rather than with any desire to dominate the stage.

But Brando's growing unease found its final expression when Jessica Tandy was replaced by Uta Hagen, and Brando refused to rehearse with the new Blanche. This may have been because Kazan had chosen not to continue with the play's direction, handing over to his old Actors' Studio colleague, Harold Clurman. Clurman, in his role as drama critic of the *New Republic*, had written a perceptive and intelligent review of *Streetcar* in which he stated that 'the play [with Brando playing the role] becomes the triumph of Stanley Kowalski: with the collusion of the audience which is no longer on the side of the angels ... Mr. Brando is tough without being irremediably coarse.' This judgement is tantamount to saying that Kazan and Brando had failed in their presentation of the play and was evidently what prompted Kazan – in a somewhat mischievous spirit – to elect Clurman as his successor.

Brando finally left the production in 1949, leaving Hagen partnered by Anthony Quinn's Kowalski, and immediately reacted against the popular and critical adulation he had garnered during his time with the play. For the first time, he began to talk seriously about making

During his protracted stay in Europe, Brando was briefly engaged to an attractive French gamine *named Josiane Berenger, daughter of a fisherman from Bandol on the French Riviera.*

films but he was not interested, he said, in the standard Hollywood product. 'I do not think that anybody connected with the films in the United States has ever made a sincere effort to avail himself of their fullest potential the way they do, say, in France,' he was quoted as saying. During his time in New York he had developed a passion for the European cinema which may perhaps have opened his eyes to the possibilities of the medium. As well as such French films as Marcel Carnés *Les Enfants du Paradis*, he was fond of the Italian neo-realists led by Rossellini and de Sica. Instead of following up the many offers that were coming his way via the MCA agency, Brando retreated to Europe in search of rest, anonymity and possibly inspiration. In Paris he was drawn to the fashionable intellectual cafe-society of the Left Bank, then in the throes of existentialism. Among those he met was the singer Juliette Greco whose repertoire included songs written by Jean-Paul Sartre and Raymond Queneau. Greco was much taken with Brando, whom she remembers as 'a very polite and charming man with a great interest in everything. But I had the impression that he was not very strong. In performance, of course, he had enormous strength so that he only had to say something for you to believe it absolutely.' To Brando's great delight, *Streetcar* was then being presented in Paris with Arletty, star of *Les Enfants du Paradis*, in the role of Blanche.

Brando presented himself at the stage door to pay his respects to one of his idols, only to find that Arletty was disapproving of his casual attire of jeans and T-shirt, believing it to be beneath the dignity of a man hailed as one of Broadway's leading actors. Brando later described the French star as 'a tough article' and dismissed his backstage visit as 'a mistake'.

After a brief tour of Italy, Brando returned to Paris where he ran into Maynard Morris, the New York agent who had arranged his audition for *I Remember Mama*. Morris contacted MCA, notifying them of Brando's Paris address in case they had any new projects on offer. Whether Brando had investigated the possibility of working in the European cinema at this time is uncertain, but he would finally achieve that ambition many years later when he acted (in impeccable French) under the direction of the Italian director Bernardo Bertolucci in *Last Tango in Paris*.

MCA did have an offer for Brando, albeit one he had already turned down while still in New York. It came from the Stanley Kramer Company and was the story of a group of paraplegic war veterans coming to terms with their injuries in the peacetime world. Kramer had established a reputation with two adaptations of work by the popular American humorist, Ring Lardner: *This is New York*, a comedy which traded heavily on Lardner's knowing mockery of city life, and *Champion*, an altogether darker piece in which Kirk Douglas starred as an unscrupulously ambitious boxer. In addition, Kramer had already tackled an army-based subject in *Home of the Brave* which took a critical look at race relations in service life. His output was far from the run-of-the-mill Hollywood fare which so displeased Brando. For this new project, Kramer had chosen the Austrian-born director, Fred Zinnemann, whose career had begun in pre-war Germany and who had recently distinguished himself with *The Search*, a sensitive treatment of the plight of displaced persons starring Montgomery Clift. The film's writer would be Kramer's regular collaborator, Carl Foreman, who would later work with Zinnemann and Kramer on the classic western, *High Noon*. On the advice of the veteran Hollywood director, Lewis Milestone, Brando decided to accept Kramer's $40,000 offer after all and returned to America from Europe to work on the film that would mark his screen debut: *The Men*.

Immediately before his trip to Hollywood, Brando prepared for the discipline of working to a camera by making his only foray into live television with *Come Out Fighting* for NBC. Once in California, however, he shunned the social side of Hollywood life and sequestered himself in Birmingham Veterans Hospital at Van Nuys where he could spend hours on the paraplegic wards studying for his role. The casting of an able-bodied actor in the role of a disabled person provides a challenge that is usually rewarded with high critical praise, borne out

Brando buying fruit in Bandol. He enjoyed the freedom of French street life and considered staying in Europe to work with European stage and film directors.

31

The love story between Wright and Brando plunged The Men *into conventional Hollywood melodrama, but the young actor was not afraid of showing the petulant and self-pitying side of his character.*

in recent years by the performances of Dustin Hoffman in *Rain Man*, Daniel Day-Lewis in *My Left Foot* and Tom Cruise in *Born on the Fourth of July*. Even in 1950, when the subject had rarely been tackled, Brando must have realised that his role was a gift for an actor wishing to make a strong first impression on screen.

The whole point of *The Men* was to give audiences a taste of the problems faced by disabled soldiers in their attempts to return to a normal life. Using the character of a forthright hospital doctor (played with no trace of sentiment by Everett Sloane), Foreman's screenplay made clear that there was no possibility of easy answers or miracle cures and that the injured men faced a long and painful period of acceptance and adjustment. Ken Wilocek's reaction to his disablement, with his initial withdrawal from his companions and rejection of the love of his fiancée, was entirely in keeping with the experience of many officers and men in his situation. Brando's task was to chart the coming to terms with reality of this proud, intelligent but otherwise unexceptional man as he learned to cope with the distressing problems of impotence and his permanent confinement to a wheelchair.

Despite its good intentions, *The Men* seems today to be less brave, and more severely compromised by the inevitable injection of 'hope', in the shape of Wilocek's unwaveringly loyal girlfriend (Teresa Wright) with whom he eventually wheels off into the sunset. This leavening of the film's didactic tone was essential at that time, even in Hollywood's independent sector, and it is a testament to the sensitivity of Zinnemann's direction and to Brando's own rigorous characterisation that *The Men* retains any power at all.

In 1950 Brando made his film debut as Ken Wilocek, the paraplegic hero of Fred Zinnemann's The Men. *Teresa Wright co-starred as his long-suffering fiancée. Here, Wilocek struggles to stand for his wedding to Wright, aided by Everett Sloane as the tough but tender doctor.*

Kramer was initially worried about the pairing of Zinnemann and Brando, fearing that the gentle Austrian might lack the necessary authority to control the reputedly mercurial actor. In fact, the two were more alike in temperament than the producer imagined, and they formed a close and fruitful partnership based on mutual trust and respect. Zinnemann admired the way Brando became so quickly attuned to film acting and he was able to encourage him to maintain a level of truth in his portrayal that makes the performance all the more impressive for its lack of any pleading for audience sympathy. Wilocek is depicted as a whole man, by turns angry, vulnerable and resilient, whose condition leaves him feeling physically and emotionally incomplete. It is a raw and honest performance and, despite Wilocek's acknowledged sexual impotence, it is charged with the erotic power that had already propelled Brando to stardom on stage. As the American critic René Jordan has written: 'Under the broken body and the childish tantrums there is a vein of iron, a suggestion of a toppled god, a maimed Apollo.' This special quality, which can be neither properly defined nor affected, would ensure that Brando's performance was regarded as more than an exceptional piece of acting but would come to be seen as a promise of a new realism – allied to the direct and unpolished style of European acting – on American screens.

The Men was, predictably, not a popular success. Despite the soft ending and the inclusion of a lush score by Dmitri Tiomkin, the film was too downbeat for the general audience. By 1950, the theme of the re-settlement of ex-servicemen was becoming familiar and its most popular example, William Wyler's *The Best Years Of Our Lives* had won five Academy Awards in 1946 and was still fresh in the public memory. Admittedly, it had focussed largely on able-bodied veterans but it did feature a character who had lost his hands in battle (played by Harold Russell, a genuinely handless veteran who won an Oscar for this, his only role). More to the point, it had stars like Myrna Loy, Frederic March, Dana Andrews and Teresa Wright playing sympathetic characters. *The Men* had Teresa Wright, but the rest of Zinnemann's cast were little-known. Arthur Jurado, a genuine paraplegic cast in the small role of Angel, was, in his own way, just as effective as Harold Russell. The sight of the boyishly handsome Jurado, whose magnificent torso testified to his interest in physical fitness, going through his paces in the film's gym scenes is remarkably poignant. But the film had the earnestness of a dramatised documentary – a post-war extension of the 'Why We Fight' series. Zinnemann had cut his Hollywood teeth on the short *Crime Does Not Pay*, which dramatised case histories of the 1930s and he had acquired a reputation for documentary realism with the *Seventh Cross* and *The Search*. His use of real paraplegics like Jurado in smallish roles only emphasized the docu-drama aspect of the film.

The critics however were unanimous in their praise of Brando. According to *Time*, Brando's 'halting, mumbled delivery, glowering silences and expert simulation of paraplegics do not suggest acting at all; they look chillingly like the real thing' while the *New York Herald-Tribune* observed that Brando relied 'entirely on understanding of character and technical virtuosity' rather than depending on the kind of personality projection that was the hallmark of Hollywood acting up to that point. The European cinema, with its regular use of non-professionals in lead roles or with stars such as the Swiss actor Michel Simon whose absorption in a role was total, had seen many examples of this 'truthful' style but for Hollywood, Brando's 'combination of style, depth and range', as *Sight and Sound* put it, came 'like a blood transfusion into cinema acting'.

The critics were not so generous to the film itself, finding it generally uneven. In fact, a small section of the film involving Brando's rival for Teresa Wright's affections had been scrapped, taking with it some of the scenes which developed Wright's character. The actor hired to play the rival was the son of one of the film's backers and his performance was so bad that it was decided to cut him out of the picture rather than risk the impolitic step of re-casting.

The Men was released in 1950, and although its reception was mixed, the Hollywood community had noticed the newcomer from Broadway. He was portrayed in the gossip columns and trade papers as a not entirely likeable eccentric. Once again, Brando's habit of masking his shyness with a facetious or clowning exterior was shaping the popular perception of him. While filming *The Men* he took great delight in allowing visitors to the Birmingham Veterans Hospital – where much of the film was shot – to believe he was a real paraplegic. He would then spring out of his wheelchair and perform

In reality, the off-screen Brando looked like any conventional young man of his generation.

an impromptu tap dance, or else weepingly praise the healing power of prayer. It was, of course, little more than an actor's way of breaking the tension during a period of intense work, but its questionable taste was grist to the mill for columnists who wished to 'colour' their copy.

From the beginning of his career, Brando nurtured a strong dislike of the show-business publicity machine, particularly such highly influential gossip-writers as Louella Parsons (whom he called 'the fat one') and Hedda Hopper (he dubbed her 'the one with the hat'). Left to his own devices, he would probably have avoided interviews altogether but he had formed a close friendship with Stanley Kramer's press agent, Jack Cooper, a man he found uncharacteristically sympathetic. It was Cooper who persuaded Brando to give his first Hollywood interviews, but Brando saw them as a tiresome process and was inclined to behave foolishly in the face of even the most innocuous questions, giving his birthplace as 'Outer Mongolia' on more than one occasion.

Brando's treatment of them as mediocrities obsessed with trivia led the Hollywood press corps to declare open war on him. At any and every opportunity, the columnists rushed to tell their readers that Brando was 'an oddball', 'a goof' or 'a crazy, mixed-up kid'. Their criteria for judging actors was simple and unimaginative: there were no good or bad actors, in their view, just those who were 'co-operative' or – the ultimate Hollywood sin – 'uncooperative'. Brando was quickly and permanently slotted into the second category. Even when he played the Hollywood rules and escorted an attractive woman to a fashionable restaurant, he met with this kind of comment from Louella Parsons: 'Marlon Brando, who was making like a well-groomed man for at least a week, reverted to type last night. He was at the Saddle and Sirloin with Dorothy Adamson – but without shoes.'

After the release of *The Men*, Brando returned to New York and to more classes at the New School for Social Research. He continued to resist offers of long-term Hollywood contracts, wishing to retain some measure of independence. Despite the press distortions, Brando had acquired a reputation for conscientious diligence on the film with Zinnemann. More film offers were swift to follow, including the chance to star opposite John Garfield in *The Harder They Fall* from the novel by Budd Schulberg (who would later script *On The Waterfront*, the most successful of Brando's early films). When Charles Feldman bought the screen rights to *A Streetcar Named Desire*, he approached Kazan to direct and Brando was naturally asked to repeat the role of Kowalski for the cinema. However, he was reluctant to do it, believing he had exhausted the possibilities of the role during the play's initial run on Broadway.

Kazan sympathised with Brando's position. He himself had had doubts about directing the film version and had complained to

Brando on 'kitchen duty' during the shooting of A Streetcar Named Desire.

37

Brando with director Elia Kazan between takes on the set of A Streetcar Named Desire.

Tennessee Williams; 'Oh, God, Tenn, it would be like marrying the same woman twice.' But now that he had come around to the idea he was determined to work with the original stage cast. Warner Brothers, who were proposing to distribute the picture, had vetoed the use of Jessica Tandy. Although she was hugely respected in the theatre, Jessica Tandy meant little to cinema audiences and Warners wanted to replace her with a star name in the role of Blanche. If Kazan came up with an acceptable name for Blanche, said Warners, he was free to use the rest of his Broadway cast. Kazan agreed and immediately re-approached Brando, who relented. He accepted the $75,000 offer and moved in to a Coldwater Canyon apartment with Elia Kazan and his wife, Molly Day Thacher – a former play reader with the Group Theatre who had first brought Tennessee Williams to Kazan's attention.

Louella Parsons could not resist another swipe at her new target: 'Marlon Brando has never been accused of being a modest violet – and here is a set of figures to prove it. For his first movie, *The Men* Stanley Kramer is paying him $50,000. For his second picture, *A Streetcar Named Desire*, he'll get $75,000. After that, he is going to ask $125,000 for his charm and talent, which is a lot of do-re-mi for a guy who arrived here with just two suits. It's a lot of moola for a guy with three suits, for that matter.'

Kazan's somewhat hesitant choice for Blanche was the English actress, Vivien Leigh. She was certainly a big enough name, as far as Warner Brothers were concerned, thanks to her starring role as Scarlett O'Hara in the hugely successful *Gone With The Wind*. She was also familiar with the part already as she had played Blanche in the first London production of *Streetcar* in 1949, under the direction of her husband Laurence Olivier. Ironically this was precisely why Kazan was uncertain about casting her in the movie version. *Streetcar*'s Broadway producer, Irene Selznick, had seen this London production which she felt was ill-conceived, an opinion she had passed on to Kazan.

The script had already been re-shaped to conform with the Hollywood Production Code, which toned down the language and all but neutered the sexual charge of the original. Two provisions embodied in the Code might have been drafted with *Streetcar* in mind: 'Adultery and rape, sometimes necessary plot material, must not be explicitly featured, or

Brando with Vivien Leigh as Blanche in the film version of Streetcar. *Like Jessica Tandy, she rose to the challenge of working with the mercurial Brando whose technique differed radically from her own.*

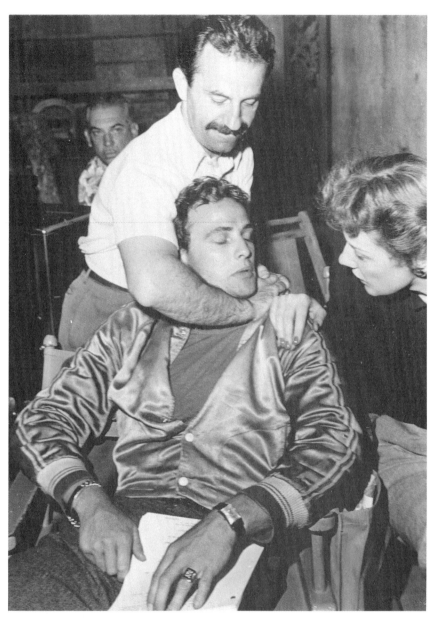

Actor Nick Dennis practises a stranglehold on Brando during an off-set moment on Streetcar. *Dennis, another member of the original Broadway cast broke Brando's nose during a 'friendly' boxing match backstage.*

justified, or presented attractively', and 'excessive and lustful kissing, lustful embraces, suggestive postures and gestures are not to be shown'. The Code had its absurd side, too. In Scene Nine of the play script, immediately after Kowalski has exposed her past, Blanche was required to scream: 'Fire! Fire! Fire!' The Code office demanded that this line be excised for fear of sending cinema patrons into a panic.

On being introduced to Brando, Vivien Leigh surprised her co-star by complimenting him on his performance in the Katherine Cornell-Guthrie McClintic *Antigone* which she had seen with Olivier back in 1946. Leigh's biographer, Anne Edwards, suggests that Brando found such politeness off-putting, perhaps because he feared it was hypocritical. It took a few days for the two stars to establish a rapport but when Brando discovered that she was being genuinely polite, he delighted Leigh with wickedly accurate impersonations of Olivier as Henry V. However, Kazan's fears were confirmed when he began directing Leigh who was inclined to interrupt him with protestations that she 'had not done it that way with Larry in London'. After two weeks, Kazan was forced to issue a strong reminder that this was not London and that he, not Olivier, was the director. This had the required result and Leigh slowly relaxed into accepting Kazan's view of Blanche. She and the director eventually became close friends and Kazan has written that Leigh 'had a small talent, but the greatest determination to succeed of any actress I've known. She'd have crawled over broken glass if she thought it would help her performance'.

With Brando and Leigh working effectively together, Kazan was at ease working with a group of actors who had formed an effective unit. Once again, Kim Hunter played Stella and Karl Malden Mitch (although Warner Brothers had tried to have James Cagney in the role). Having accustomed himself to film work on *The Men*, Brando was able to bring to the screen a great deal of the dangerous quality that had made his stage performance so outstanding. His practice of attacking each scene afresh was ideally suited to the camera: he would not be locked in endless repetition here. He exploited every opportunity to the full, raising the temperature of every scene he entered. No matter that the script was bowdlerised, no matter that the film ends (unlike the play) with Stella rejecting Stanley, Brando did nothing to dilute the carnality of his performance. So powerful is the sexual chemistry between Brando and Hunter that when her rejection of him does come, you know it won't last more than a minute. As a result, the film is one of the most satisfying screen versions ever made of a Broadway play.

Even after the restrictions of the Production Code had been satisfied, the completed film ran into trouble with the Catholic Legion of Decency, which gave it a 'C' – for 'Condemned' – rating, a possible threat to future bookings. Despite Kazan's protests, Warner Brothers made cuts in the film – including the removal of a section of the musical score which was deemed 'too carnal' – and *Streetcar* finally opened in September 1951.

Review after review confirmed what his performance in *The Men* had made common knowledge in Hollywood, that Brando was an extraordinary new screen talent. The *New York Herald-Tribune* hailed 'a remarkably truthful performance of a heavy-muscled, practical

Brando on the set of Streetcar *(top) with the improvised shower which was the source of Stanley Kowalski's all-important sweaty appearance. The film of* Streetcar *re-informed Brando's identification with the role of Kowalski (above).*

animal, secure in the normalcy of marriage and friendship, cunning but insensitive, aware of Blanche's deceits but not of her suffering. This performance is as close to perfect as one could wish'. Those who had seen his stage portrayal were not disappointed for, as Bosley Crowther noted in the *New York Times*, he had 'all the energy and steel-spring characteristics that made him vivid on the stage. But here, where we're closer to him, he seems that much more highly charged, his despairs seem that much more pathetic and his comic moments that much more slyly enjoyed'. The *Observer* found Brando's Kowalski 'exacts the same sort of pity as Caliban' and praised 'one of the strongest and most selfless performances I remember seeing in the cinema'. Hollis Alpert in the *Saturday Review* was no less fulsome: 'Marlon Brando, who immediately became our most talented young actor with his legitimate performance of the Stanley Kowalski role, enlarges it in the film version to seem even more shocking, to have more facets'. *Time* magazine made *Streetcar* a cover story but its assertion that 'where Barrymore was "The Great Profile", Valentino "The Sheik" and Clark Gable "The King", Marlon Brando is... "The Slob" ' gave unwanted currency to the views of the Hollywood scandal sheets.

Nevertheless, with the critical success of the film matched by healthy box office returns, Brando had broken into that realm of popularity that made his 1951 Oscar nomination inevitable. In the event, he would lose out to Humphrey Bogart, for his portrayal of the stoker in *The African Queen*. Vivien Leigh, however, was awarded an Oscar for Best Actress for her portrayal of Blanche, although her performance seems overly theatrical today, while Brando's remains fresh. Karl Malden and Kim Hunter also got Oscars for their supporting roles. Elia Kazan was nominated for Best Director but lost to George Stevens whose *A Place in the Sun* was *Streetcar's* strongest rival for the Best Picture Award. In the event, the Gershwin musical *An American in Paris* won out over both dramas.

Despite missing out on the Oscar, Brando found himself pushed to the front rank of Hollywood stars after only his second film. Newspapers and magazines junked the studio pictures of the young actor in collar and tie and reprinted production stills from *Streetcar* showing him in the torn, sweaty T-shirt and blue jeans which were closer to his off-screen apparel. The gossip sheets filled up with stories about Hollywood's 'misfit', capitalising on his distaste for interviews. Louella Parsons, never an original wit, wrote lengthy columns about 'The Slob'. Even his enemies had to admit that Marlon Brando was hot. When he had made his first film newspapers joked about 'Marlon of the Movies' – a reference to Henry Leon Wilson's comic novel, 'Merton of the Movies'. It was intended as mockery; in the space of a year Brando had turned it into reality.

Brando as Stanley Kowalski in Streetcar. *Hollywood gossips had not been so scandalised by an actor's on-screen dress sense since Clark Gable took off his shirt in the thirties comedy* It Happened One Night.

3

In search
of a role

Elia Kazan directs Brando and Jean Peters on the set of Viva Zapata! *(above). Brando as Johnny in* The Wild One *(right). Despite its obvious and soft-centred 'message', the film was banned in the UK for twelve years.*

IMMEDIATELY before *Streetcar* Kazan had been preparing two other film scripts. One of these was *The Hook*, a waterfront drama scripted by Arthur Miller, whose plays *All My Sons* and *Death of a Salesman* Kazan had directed with great success on Broadway. The other was a screen treatment of the life of the Mexican revolutionary leader Emiliano Zapata which Kazan had been trying to realise since 1944 and for which the novelist John Steinbeck had written a script. The subject was guaranteed to appeal to Brando whose earlier defence of underdogs was developing into a concern for the rights of oppressed peoples, and readily agreed to work on the film with Kazan. As soon as the shooting of *Streetcar* was completed, Kazan set out to film *Viva Zapata!* with Darryl F. Zanuck of Twentieth-Century Fox as producer.

Steinbeck and Kazan had already encountered problems in attempting to shoot the film in Mexico as they could not get their script past the Mexican National Censor. In a conciliatory mood, Steinbeck – who had been in Mexico for the filming of his novel *The Pearl* – identified the root of the problem. An American director shooting a film in English with an American actor playing one of Mexico's greatest heroes was a little like a Mexican crew turning up in Illinois to film the Abraham Lincoln story with a Mexican leading man. On the other hand, Kazan was convinced that the Mexicans would have agreed if the story had been given a communist slant. In any event, they were forced to settle for the Texas borderlands.

Now Zanuck placed another obstacle in their path. As *Streetcar* had not yet been released, he did not feel that Brando was sufficiently well-known for the role of Zapata, and Zanuck wanted Tyrone Power or Anthony Quinn instead. Kazan managed to persuade him to allow Brando to test for the role in a short scene with Julie Harris, whom

Kazan wanted for the role of Zapata's wife. Miss Harris was fresh from her success as Frankie in the Broadway adaptation of Carson McCullers' novella, *The Member of the Wedding*, but the sight of her and Brando as a couple of Mexicans did not convince Zanuck. Miss Harris was out of the question; as for Brando, Zanuck cabled Kazan: 'I DON'T UNDERSTAND A GODDAMNED THING THE SON OF A BITCH SAYS. CAN'T YOU STOP HIM FROM MUMBLING?' Kazan persisted; he brought in a dialogue coach and make-up man to 'latinise' Brando and selected Jean Peters, a suitably dark studio contract player, to play opposite him. This time the producer relented and filming got under way.

Brando's price had by now gone up to $100,000 and he relished the chance to make his first film to involve location shooting. In preparation for the role, he travelled to Sonora, Mexico, to study the Mexican people at close hand. No such preparation was necessary for Anthony Quinn who, having been passed up for the leading part, was compensated by being cast as Zapata's brother, Eufemio. Despite his Irish name, Quinn was of Mexican origin and his first-hand knowledge of the country was to prove invaluable to Kazan for whom he acted as an unofficial technical adviser. The potential for friction between Marlon Brando and Anthony Quinn was enormous, and Kazan was not alone in fearing it. Not only did Quinn know that he had been the producer's preferred choice for the lead role, but he had also taken over from Brando as Kowalski in the Broadway production of *Streetcar* to excellent reviews, and remained in the part for two years – six months longer than Brando.

Kazan is snide about Harold Clurman's production of *Streetcar* in his autobiography; he describes Quinn, slightingly, as 'an actor amenable to being led; he listens like a child'. In point of fact, some influential critics preferred Clurman's production to Kazan's, and Quinn's performance to Brando's. Here is Eric Bentley: 'Quinn's achievement is negative but substantial: he cuts down the number of laughs that his lines can register in order to be more loyal to the play's meaning. Stanley is brutal, and Marlon Brando was quite wrong for the part. Brando has muscular arms, but his eyes give them the lie. Not discouraged, perhaps, by Kazan, he gave us an Odets character: Stanley Kowalski of Brooklyn whose tough talk is but the mask of a suffering, sensitive soul.' Bentley goes on to compare productions, supporting Clurman's assertion that Kazan and Brando distorted the play's meaning to favour Kowalski – thus glamourising a brute. For Bentley, Clurman's production got closer to Williams. Bentley concludes: 'On the whole Marlon Brando's performance was just a tour-de-force: a rather feminine actor overinterpreting a masculine role. Yet when Anthony Quinn portrays Kowalski as an illiterate we are surprised at some of the big words he uses.'

Yet it was with Brando that the character of Kowalski was popularly identified. It was almost inevitable therefore that Quinn would feel some resentment towards his younger co-star and was probably particularly sensitive to any suspicion of partiality. Within days of starting work on *Viva Zapata!* Quinn was complaining that Kazan had a tendency to favour Brando in his direction. On the contrary, Kazan argued, his direction of Brando was extremely minimal. Finding Brando's instincts to be wholly in tune with the character, Kazan barely uttered a word of direction – his watchword with Brando was: 'If it isn't broke, don't fix it.' Quinn was unconvinced and still felt aggrieved. Finally, Kazan sent Brando to talk with him and the two actors eventually formed a close working friendship.

Brando as the Mexican rebel leader in the ill-starred John Steinbeck/Elia Kazan collaboration Viva Zapata!

Viva Zapata! was conceived as a rather grandiose historical epic through which Kazan could portray the 'relationship between abstract politics and personal character' but it failed for a variety of reasons.

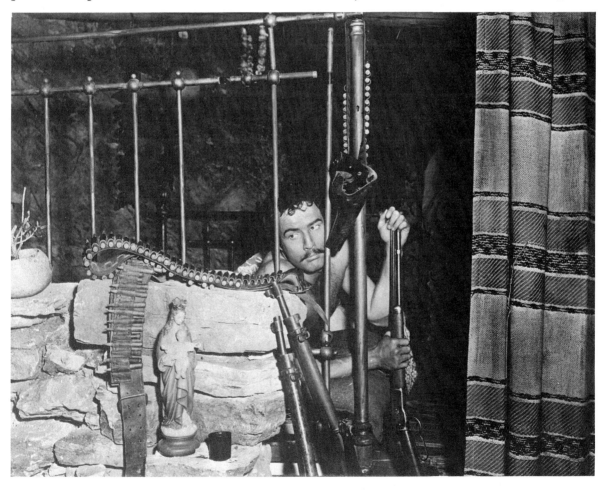

Brando and Anthony Quinn were cast as brothers in Viva Zapata! *There were initially tensions between them on set as Quinn, who was half-Mexican, had been passed over for the main role.*

Not the least of these was Kazan's own proximity to the hysterical anti-communist feeling that was building up within the American film industry as a prelude to the shameful 'investigations' of the House Un-American Activities Committee. His connection with the Group Theatre had brought Kazan into contact with many of the most radically-minded writers and actors of that time. Many of them would, like him, go on to work in the cinema and television where their social commitment generated an atmosphere of creative energy and change. Equally, many of Kazan's colleagues had joined him as card-carrying Communists during the 'thirties when the Party seemed to be the only organisation prepared to take a stand against Fascism.

The Zapata story had already been 'cleansed' of moral impurities – Zapata's twenty-six 'wives' were condensed into one, played with proper modesty by Jean Peters. Now Steinbeck (whose reputation had been built on the socially didactic masterpiece, *The Grapes of Wrath*) worked on shaping a script that was 'untainted' by the leftist perspective so feared by the Hollywood establishment. The film portrays Zapata as a poor-but-honest man who leads a peasants' revolt against his country's dictator, President Diaz, joining forces in the process with the Texas-based revolutionary, Francisco Madero. The dictator is defeated but Madero is subsequently assassinated leaving Zapata as the reluctant ruler of his people. Once in power, Zapata discovers its corrupting influence, which culminates dramatically in the peasants' denunciation of his brother as a tyrannical oppressor. Thoroughly disillusioned, Zapata steps down and walks complacently into the 'purifying' death of a peasants' ambush. These events take place over a period of twenty years and the story's underlying moral would seem to be that power leads inevitably to total corruption and the struggle for social change is not worth the candle. What the film really proves is that Kazan's urgent desire to distance himself from his left-wing past was already beginning to drain his work of vitality and truth.

In a letter to the *Saturday Review* in 1952, Kazan wrote: 'It is human character, above all, which concerns a director, writer, producer, and it was the character of Zapata which intrigued us all.' The development of that character against a background of startling political events would be a challenge for any actor, no matter how sharp his instincts. The great silent screen actress Louise Brooks, whose subtle intelligence before the camera fully matched Brando's, was once quoted as saying: 'The great art of films does not consist of descriptive movement of face and body, but in the movements of thought and soul transmitted in a kind of intense isolation.' Compare this illuminating observation with the one piece of direction Kazan does admit to giving Brando: 'A peasant does not reveal what he thinks. Things happen to him and he shows no reaction. He knows if he shows certain reactions he'll be marked "bad" and be killed.' Thus Brando, be-wigged and moustachioed, his eyes slanted and skin darkened by the make-up department, was encouraged to adopt the inpenetrable gaze that characterised his performance. As *The Men* and *Streetcar* had revealed, Brando was blessed with enormous presence on screen and his Zapata was no less watchable. However, the lingering impression was of an enigma being strongly presented but never examined. Of course, Brando took every opportunity to step outside the near impossible restrictions of his role, notably in the scenes with Jean Peters, but he was ill-served by the director who knew him best.

For all its shortcomings, *Viva Zapata!* still led to Brando being named Best Actor at the 1952 Cannes Film Festival and gaining his second Oscar nomination. Ironically, he lost this time to Gary Cooper in *High Noon*, the most successful film made by the same team responsible for *The Men*. Anthony Quinn, however, won the award for Best Supporting Actor for his more relaxed and convincing portrayal of Zapata's brother. The critical reaction to the film was muted but respectful and, while *Viva Zapata!* failed at the box office, Brando and Kazan did at least emerge with their reputations intact.

Still free from contractual obligations, Brando was able to sift through the offers that were now pouring in for him at MCA. Among these was a request from Fred Zinnemann for Brando to play Van Gogh in a film biography and a major European offer

Brando made an audition tape to convince Hollywood backers that he could play Mark Antony in Joseph L. Mankiewicz's film of Julius Caesar. *His performance in the film assuaged all doubts. A dummy stands in for the 'assassinated' Louis Calhern (above) as Brando rehearses Antony's speech over the stricken Caesar.*

of a script by the leading Italian neo-realist Cesare Zavattini. This would be *Stazione Termini* with Ingrid Bergman as co-star, under the direction of the veteran French film-maker, Claude Autant-Lara. Autant-Lara had been a major force in French cinema since the silent era but his career would come to an abrupt halt during the heyday of the French New Wave. Although Brando was determined to extend himself as much as possible, he nevertheless turned down both of these offers. David O. Selznick later optioned the Zavattini script for his wife, Jennifer Jones, and it was made with Jones and Montgomery Clift. As for Van Gogh, he would be portrayed by Kirk Douglas in Vincente Minnelli's respectful but interesting *Lust For Life*. The man who eventually produced Minnelli's film was John Houseman and in 1952 he, too, was eager to secure Marlon Brando's services. Houseman's project was a film of Shakespeare's *Julius Caesar* to be directed by Joseph L. Mankiewicz.

John Houseman was based at MGM but his tastes were famously at odds with those of most film producers. Born Jacques Haussmann, he was a Romanian of Alsatian/Jewish/Celtic origin who had begun a career in the grain business only to lose his $20,000-a-year job during the Wall Street Crash of 1929. Turning his attention to the theatre, he distinguished himself in a fruitful partnership with Orson Welles, with whom he founded the Mercury Theatre Company. Their productions of the 'Voodoo' *Macbeth*, *The Cradle Will Rock* and the famous radio version of *The War of the Worlds* had earned them acclaim as well as notoriety and brought many Hollywood offers, culminating in Welles' debut feature, *Citizen Kane* (1941). After this Houseman moved on to other theatre and film ventures before accepting a position at MGM. He had already found most of his *Julius Caesar* cast when he had what he called the 'mad but brilliant idea' of approaching Brando to play Mark Antony.

Houseman cabled Mankiewicz, who was in London meeting with John Gielgud, who had signed to play Cassius, and asked him to delay setting up a film test for Paul Scofield, a prospective Antony. Mankiewicz agreed, but expressed scepticism about Brando's ability to handle the demands of Shakespeare. Invited to test for the part, Brando declined but offered instead to make a tape recording of one of Antony's speeches. The one he chose was not the celebrated funeral oration but Antony's entrance into the Senate immediately after the assassination of Caesar, the speech ends with his demand for vengeance: 'Cry havoc, and let slip the dogs of war!' The tape confirmed Houseman's belief that this was the actor he needed. He had already rejected the studio's demands to cast the roles entirely with British actors – if that were to be the case, he argued, the film might just as well be made in England. Mankiewicz was equally impressed with the tape and immediately shelved his doubts on the matter.

When Mankiewicz assembled his cast for the first read-though his doubts must surely have returned. Alongside Gielgud and Brando were James Mason as Brutus; Deborah Kerr as his wife, Portia; Louis Calhern as Caesar; Greer Garson as Calpurnia, Caesar's wife, and Edmond O'Brien as Brutus. Apart from Gielgud who read with consummate ease, none of the principals was particularly inspiring. Houseman recalled that Mason was 'depressed and embarrassed' by Gielgud's brilliance and read his entire role while chewing on a pipe, Garson was 'very British and ladylike', O'Brien and Kerr were 'adequate', while Calhern read with 'the meaningless flamboyance of a nineteenth-century provincial ham'. But the focus of attention was bound to be Brando, whom Houseman remembered as giving 'a perfect performance as a stuttering bumpkin only remotely acquainted with the English language'. It was known that Brando had become friendly with Laurence Olivier after working with Vivien Leigh in *Streetcar*, and a Hollywood rumour suggested that the voice on Brando's audition tape

Brando impressed co-stars and critics alike with his performance as Antony. One commentator suggested that to appreciate Brando's versatility one should try to imagine John Gielgud portraying Stanley Kowalski (in Streetcar*).*

51

was actually that of the great Shakespearean actor. Mankiewicz knew this to be nonsense, but it was obvious to all concerned that *Julius Caesar* was going to be a real challenge.

Mankiewicz demanded a three-week, on-set rehearsal period. It was an intelligent decision, but hitherto unheard of in a film studio. Justifiably regarded as an 'actor's director', Mankiewicz was confident and patient enough to work his cast towards a production worthy of their talents. He was helped enormously by Gielgud, returning to the screen after ten years to make his first American film. Word-perfect in his own role from the beginning, Gielgud – an unusually generous actor – set about boosting the confidence of his colleagues. Brando willingly turned himself over to Gielgud's tuition and, when it came to the filming, he tirelessly performed his difficult Forum speech for take after take; even when the camera was on the crowd of extras he was uncomplaining, speaking his lines at performance pitch. 'Brando', Gielgud recalled, 'was greatly hampered by the fact that he did not know how the scenes were placed by Shakespeare or how they progressed from one climax to another. Brando was very self-conscious and modest, it seemed to me. He would come on to the set in his fine, tomato-coloured toga, his hair cropped in a straight fringe, expecting to find someone making fun of his appearance. I had only one scene with him in the film. We went through the speeches in the morning ... and I made some suggestions. The next morning...I found that he had taken note of everything I had said and spoke the lines exactly as I had suggested.'

Mankiewicz later called Gielgud in to see the rushes of Mark Antony's speech over Caesar's body which the director thought Brando had done 'absolutely marvellously'. Gielgud was not impressed. 'I thought he was giving a bad imitation of Olivier, but it was hardly my place to say so. I never met Brando again, which was a pity because I felt that he was enormously responsive. I thought he would have made a wonderful Oedipus.' At their last meeting, Gielgud 'begged' Brando to play Hamlet as part of a classical season, shared with Paul Scofield and Gielgud himself, at the Lyric Theatre, Hammersmith, in London. Brando, perhaps unsure that he could produce a comparable performance in the very different theatrical discipline, declined. He was already committed, he explained, to a scuba-diving holiday in the Bahamas. In any case, he said, he never wanted to go back to the theatre.

The cast benefited further from another Mankiewicz innovation – he shot the film as near as possible, in sequence. By the time they reached the difficult Battle of Philippi (the only disappointing section, looking as it does like a standard Western ambush), Houseman and Mankiewicz knew that they had achieved their ambition, to make a creditable American film version of Shakespeare.

The critical reception bore out their confidence and confirmed their belief in Brando. *The Observer*'s critic in London suggested that, in order to appreciate Brando's versatility, one should try to imagine Gielgud in *Streetcar*. *Variety*'s reaction was typical: 'Any fears about Brando appearing in Shakespeare are dispelled by his compelling portrayal as the revengeful Mark Antony, in which he turns in the performance of his career. His interpretation of the famous funeral oration will be a conversation piece. The entire speech takes on a new light as voiced by Brando.' In fact, when Brando performed the speech to camera he received the rare accolade of whole-hearted applause from the assembled cast and crew.

For the third year in succession, Brando earned an Oscar nomination but even this did not reflect his real achievement. He had demonstrated that he was far from 'The Slob' of popular repute, he was a serious actor with an enviable range. It seemed that he had broken away from the image that was being created of him. The 1953 Oscar went to William Holden for *Stalag 17* but Brando now received a rush of film offers including the title role in Billy Wilder's projected film of *Pal Joey* and the male lead in the remake of *A Star Is Born*. He turned these down along with many other interesting proposals and signed instead to make a film which would undo most of the work he had done as Mark Antony.

Brando as the rebellious biker Johnny in Stanley Kramer's production of The Wild One; *here with Yvonne Doughty as Britches.*

The new film was inspired by an article written by Frank Rooney and published in *Harper's* magazine. It was a brutal story of two motorcycle gangs who clash in a small town and terrorise the inhabitants. Brando was first attracted to the project because of the involvement of Stanley Kramer – now based at Columbia Pictures – as producer. Kramer had been going through a difficult period at Columbia and desperately needed a financial success to match his previous film for the studio, *The Caine Mutiny*. Brando was now a star and his name on the film would guarantee Columbia's backing. Perhaps as a gesture of thanks for Kramer's early confidence in him, Brando agreed to the project before a script had been completed. It had all the hallmarks of a 'social issue' picture comparable to *The Men*, but this time Zinnemann would not be the director as he had turned down Kramer's invitation. The film had been given a working title, 'The Cyclists' Raid', and Kramer had signed the Hungarian-born Laslo Benedek to direct from a script by Ben Maddow. Benedek had worked with Kramer before, on the unsatisfactory screen version of Arthur Miller's *Death of a Salesman*, while Maddow had written John Huston's highly regarded film of *The Asphalt Jungle*.

As the project developed, Maddow was replaced by John Paxton whose work included *Fourteen Hours*, a gripping study of a crowd's reaction to an attempted suicide, starring Richard Basehart. According to the director Joseph Strick, Kramer was pressured into dropping Maddow when the screenwriter was named as a possible communist.

The Wild One *scenes in which the confused Johnny strives to explain himself to a sympathetic young woman, Mary Murphy, are ineptly written and often draw laughs from modern audiences.*

Brando approached his new role with customary dedication. He visited Hollister, the Californian town that was the scene of the events detailed in the original magazine story, and acquainted himself with the habits and fashions of motorcycle gangs. But by the time shooting began on Columbia's back lot the script had been fatally compromised to comply with the demands of the Production Code and to remove all traces of the 'communistic' influence it found inherent in the script's exploration of the gang mentality. Brando protested that this was not now the film he had signed to make, but loyalty to Kramer made him carry on.

It was the Columbia chief, Harry Cohn, who changed the film's title to *The Wild One*. This was a reference to Brando's character, Johnny, who leads the Blind Rebels Motorcycle Club in to a small American town where they gather in the local cafe. There Johnny meets Kathie (the film's 'love interest') played by Mary Murphy.

Brando felt that Paxton's dialogue for this important first scene rang false and so asked Benedek if he could improvise, with Murphy joining in for her responses. Benedek, a sympathetic and helpful director, consented and the scene is very effective, displaying the ease with which Brando absorbed his preparatory research. He establishes Johnny with a physical and vocal economy that is compelling, laying claim to the girl, the town and the film all at once.

Brando's performance is the only thing that makes *The Wild One* worth watching today. Johnny's rival, whose gang rides into town and challenges the Blind Rebels, was played by Lee Marvin. Marvin, then still a character 'heavy', is hampered by the fact that he looks too old for the part. Nor can he compete with Brando's undeniable glamour. With the film now reduced to nothing more than a standard action picture – a B-Western with motorbikes – Brando has no option but to turn in a 'star' performance, the kind of thing that had been saving Hollywood pictures for years. For the first time in his career, Brando found he had no currency but himself. True, the personality he was trying to project was Johnny's, but in this context it was perceived as his own. Ironically, the columnist Louella Parsons had only recently been moved to change her opinion of Brando. After a visit to the set of *Julius Caesar*, she wrote: 'Though his favourite reply to questions is

The Wild One: *If Brando at 30 looked silly playing the kind of 'mixed-up kid' role normally associated with his rival and imitator James Dean, Lee Marvin (as the rival gang leader seen here struggling with Brando) looked positively middle-aged.*

a noncommittal grunt, it is my private opinion that Marlon is the finest actor among the younger group. I have a feeling he would agree with me. And why not? Heifetz knows he can play the violin. Hemingway knows he can write...I think this young radical (*not* Red) could tackle just about anything in the acting field.' This scratching, mumbling, inarticulate rebel of *The Wild One* was perilously close to Parson's previous depiction of the private Brando; it was the apotheosis of 'The Slob'.

In the film's most quoted exchange, Johnny is asked what he is rebelling against; he replies, famously: 'What've you got?' The remark is facetious and only serves to underline the film's bathos. Brando did not hide his unhappiness with the result. 'I think it was a failure,' he would comment. 'We started out to do something worthwhile, to explain the psychology of the hipster. But somewhere along the way we went off the track. The result was that instead of finding why young people tend to bunch into groups that seek expression in violence, all that we did was show the violence.'

Brando did not blame Kramer or Benedek; he knew that the censors had been responsible for vitiating the project. As a final *coup de grâce* the censors further insisted on Brando, as Johnny, voicing an off-screen introduction to the film indicating that the events portrayed constituted an isolated incident. This ran counter to the script's intentions and enraged Brando who complied, but mockingly adopted an exaggerated drawl. In an age when the supposed corrupting influence of rock and roll was beginning to make headlines. *The Wild One* was accorded a notoriety which ensured its box office success and burdened Brando with an inaccurate but enduring image. The British censors took an even more extreme view and banned the film outright, denying it general exhibition until 1968.

Disenchanted with the whole experience, Brando returned to the theatre. But this was far from the comeback his admirers may have hoped for. Rather than risk a return to the competitive world of Broadway, he surrounded himself with a number of old friends William Redfield , Phil Rhodes, Carlo Fiore and others, and mounted a production of Shaw's comedy, *Arms and the Man* on a short tour of New England. Brando played the role of Sergius with William Redfield in the more rewarding part of Bluntschli. In his 1966 book, *Letters From An Actor*, Redfield remembered the production and described Brando as being 'brilliant once or twice a week, usually when nervous or otherwise disturbed. The remainder of the performances he threw away. When I occasionally complained, he would say gently, "Man, don't you get it? This is *Summer Stock*!" '

Redfield was a long-time friend and admirer of Brando but, in his view, the Brando who played opposite him in 1953 was no longer the man who ignited Broadway in *Streetcar*; he was bored and totally

indifferent to the audience 'unless it contained Adlai Stevenson or Pandit Nehru'. The Brando that Redfield describes is a man who knows that he has lost the necessary edge to carry him through a stage performance, a man who – as an actor – 'must be either forgotten or fondly remembered'. It is a damning indictment, and one that fails to give proper credit to Brando's achievement as a film actor – in fact, Redfield seems to consider acting for the camera to be a less worthy profession. It is quite possible that Brando undertook the Shaw play (for which he hand-picked the company) as a kind of relaxation after the rigours of Shakespeare and the bitter disappointment of *The Wild One*. Nevertheless the experience may have left its mark on him. He would never again set foot on a theatrical stage.

When *Arms and the Man* closed Brando and Redfield took a brief holiday in Europe, after which Brando returned cautiously to Hollywood. But, if *The Wild One* was to enshrine his popular image, his next role would confirm all the promise of his earlier work and reveal him at the height of his talent as an exemplary cinema actor.

Universal's Talent School: Brando (seated centre) gives a talk to the young hopefuls, including Clint Eastwood (standing, centre) and David Janssen (seated, at Brando's left).

57

4

The contender

HOLLYWOOD in the early 'fifties was overshadowed by one of the most dismal episodes in American domestic politics: the hearings before the House Committee on UnAmerican Activities (universally known as HUAC). With the United States and the Soviet Union ideologically polarised, the scene was set for the 'Cold War' and many left-liberal writers, actors and directors would find their careers in ruins as America's anti-communist paranoia took hold.

Congressional hearings into the 'communist influence' on Hollywood's output began in 1947 and resulted in the jailing of ten screenwriters and directors who were dubbed 'the Unfriendly Ten' for their refusal to co-operate with the Committee. They became more popularly known as 'the Hollywood Ten' and their prosecution for contempt of Congress when they invoked the First Amendment to justify their silence was a *cause célèbre* in the film industry. Hearings were suspended while the case against the Ten was pursued and, by the time they were re-opened in 1951, the situation was further dramatised by the trials of the State Department official Alger Hiss (jailed for perjury) and Julius and Ethel Rosenberg (executed as Soviet spies). The climate was one of near-hysteria and the major film studios took to operating a 'blacklist' of employees with suspected communist sympathies. This blacklist was unofficial and, for the most part, unacknowledged but it brought an abrupt end to scores of promising and established careers.

The period was dominated by the figure of Joseph McCarthy, a junior senator from Wisconsin, who seemed driven by a combination of xenophobia and self-aggrandisement in his zealous pursuit of 'Soviet intrigue' in all aspects of American life. In truth, McCarthy was merely riding the crest of a wave that was already in motion when he came

'A pigeon for a pigeon'. The script for On the Waterfront *is full of epithets for 'informer'. Brando as Terry Malloy faces the consequences of 'turning State's evidence'.*

to prominence in 1951. His downfall three years later, censured by the Senate for financial irregularities, did not stop the blacklist; the spirit of what became known as McCarthyism ran deep and would long outlive the senator himself.

Looking back on that time, the blacklisted screenwriter Dalton Trumbo (one of the Hollywood Ten) remarked: 'It will do no good to search for villains or heroes or saints or devils because there were none; there were only victims.' Despite Trumbo's caveat, there was little evidence of victimisation among those who co-operated with the Committee. Some were genuinely torn between loyalty to friends or to country, others were motivated simply by the need to maintain their own steady employment, but there was no shortage of people willing to 'name names', providing further additions to the studio blacklist.

If Brando himself escaped the Committee's attention – his social conscience had not yet found expression in political activism – several of his former colleagues did not. Stanley Kramer had already yielded to the blacklist over Ben Maddow; although in Kramer's defence it must be said that he later employed the blacklisted actor and writer Ned Young, who co-scripted (pseudonymously) two Kramer films: *The Defiant Ones* (for which Young won an Oscar) and *Inherit the Wind*. Carl Foreman, who had written *The Men*, was accused of planting a 'communist sub-text' in his screenplay for *High Noon* and – in common with many others – was forced to leave America to find work elsewhere. On the other hand, Brando's mentor Elia Kazan bowed to pressure and 'named names' of colleagues with left-wing sympathies, among them his old friend John Garfield. Kazan's position as an informer has shadowed his work ever since, but never more pointedly than in his next collaboration with Brando.

Kazan's testimony came in 1953 while Brando was shooting *Julius Caesar* for Joseph L. Mankiewicz. Brando was deeply distressed to find Kazan capable of so shameful an act and turned for guidance to Mankiewicz, whose political position was strongly opposed to Kazan's. Mankiewicz comforted Brando and advised him to remember that Kazan had been his friend and that he should not 'side with the crazies' on the matter. Nevertheless, Brando was uncertain about the thought of working with Kazan in the future.

One man who did break with Kazan at this point was Arthur Miller, who had been working on the script of *The Hook* for the director. Miller and Kazan had been a successful team in the New York theatre, where Kazan had directed the first productions of Miller's plays *All My Sons* and *Death of a Salesman*. They were looking to repeat their success in the cinema.

The Hook centred on the gangland domination of New York's waterfront, and Miller had researched the script exhaustively. He drew a great deal on the story of Pete Panto, a young longshoreman who had mysteriously disappeared while trying to lead a movement of dockers against their corrupt union president, Joe Ryan. Panto's struggle had been taken up by a group of left-wing workers who were attempting to rid the union of its connections with crooked politicians and organised crime. Miller had been helped in this research by a series of articles which appeared in *The New York Sun* newspaper under the title 'Crime on the Waterfront' and which had won a Pulitzer Prize for the newspaperman Malcolm Johnson.

Before Kazan testified to HUAC, he and Miller had had a series of meetings with Harry Cohn, the head of Columbia Pictures, who had expressed an interest in the project. Cohn, sensitive to the political climate of the time, wanted the racketeers to be replaced by communists, a change which Miller found unacceptable. Kazan, however, was keen to continue distancing himself from his left-wing past, as he had done with *Viva Zapata!* Faced with a virtual impasse at Columbia, Miller and Kazan went their separate ways with other projects. Then Kazan's HUAC testimony forced the two men irrevocably apart and plans to film *The Hook* were completely abandoned. Miller himself came before HUAC – as an unfriendly witness – in 1956. He was tried and convicted of contempt of Congress and, before winning an appeal, he was eloquently defended in the pages of *Esquire* magazine. Ironically, the author of the *Esquire* article was John Steinbeck – Kazan's screenwriter on *Viva Zapata!*

Meanwhile, Malcolm Johnson's articles had also fired the imagination of the novelist and screenwriter Budd Schulberg, who had, quite independently, written a script along the same lines under the working title of *The Bottom of the River*. Schulberg had also been a 'friendly' witness before the Committee, largely because he resented the communist-led fashion for socialist realism which had found many vociferous advocates within the writers' union. According to Schulberg, some influential critics who had initially praised his Hollywood novel *What Makes Sammy Run*, and who, like he had been, were members of the Communist Party, had been put under serious pressure to reverse their opinions. Schulberg had resigned from the Party when it became clear that his colleagues disapproved of his story about the scheming Sammy Glick who uses people mercilessly in his route to Hollywood success. This was seen as a negative view of Hollywood's working population, taking no account of the progressive elements in the studio guilds. It was also accused of being anti-semitic. Kazan, dismayed at being unable to film Miller's script, was quick to join forces with Schulberg. In 1953, they set about approaching Hollywood studios with the new screenplay.

Political considerations apart, studio bosses at that time were keen to woo audiences away from the growing competition presented by television. This meant a greater concentration on colour and spectacle.

Darryl F. Zanuck at Twentieth-Century Fox began by showing some interest in Kazan's new project but, finally, the idea of producing a film with the drab, unappealing 'realism' of Schulberg's script seemed at odds with Fox's commitment to the new process of Cinemascope.

At this point, Kazan and Schulberg were joined by the independent producer Sam Spiegel (then known as S. P. Eagle) who had enjoyed a recent success with his production of *The African Queen*. Spiegel had the idea of taking the project to United Artists and offering it as a vehicle for Frank Sinatra. Sinatra had been born in Hoboken, New Jersey where the film was to be set and, more importantly, he had become newly bankable after winning an Oscar for his supporting role in *From Here To Eternity*. Kazan found this an excellent piece of casting and began to arrange costume fittings for Sinatra.

But then, suddenly, Spiegel changed tack. He managed to talk Harry Cohn into taking the film for Columbia, despite Cohn's earlier rejection of *The Hook*. However, Columbia was not prepared to take too big a financial gamble on Sinatra and would only guarantee a budget of $500,000. When Spiegel proposed dropping Sinatra in favour of Brando, the studio offered to double the amount.

When Spiegel outlined his new proposal to Elia Kazan, the director was doubtful. He felt that he had a moral obligation to Sinatra and could see no reason to suppose that Brando would react any more favourably than Miller had to Kazan's HUAC testimony. Sam Spiegel met Brando who made it clear that he did disapprove of Kazan's Testimony but he would agree to do the film on one condition – that he be allowed to leave the location at four o'clock each afternoon so that he could meet with Bela Mittleman, his analyst in Manhattan. Kazan, who had introduced Brando to Dr. Mittleman, readily agreed. 'I always preferred Brando to anybody,' he would say later. Sinatra was out, Brando was in, and the film's title was changed to *On The Waterfront*. *On The Waterfront* was a badly flawed project from the start, because it was conceived by Elia Kazan as a grandiose justification for naming names to HUAC. Both he and Budd Schulberg were frequently attacked by their colleagues for incriminating their friends and felt they were allies in adversity. And Brando's co-star, Lee J. Cobb, cast in the role of the corrupt union boss, ironically called Johnny Friendly, had also been a 'friendly' witness. He had named names for expediency, however, not from conviction. It was all very well, he claimed, for blacklisted writers to continue working under pseudonyms but actors could not change their faces. As if to give weight to Cobb's view, the blacklisted actor Zero Mostel once observed sadly, 'I am a man of a thousand faces – all of them blacklisted.'

The more Kazan worked on the script with Schulberg, the further *On The Waterfront* moved from being the story of dockland corruption and the concerted action that ended it; instead it became a melodramatic

Brando's parents visit him on the set of On the Waterfront. *From left to right, Marlon Brando Snr.; the film's producer Sam Spiegel; Dorothy Pennebaker Brando (who was to die shortly afterwards) and Brando.*

allegory of Kazan's position as an informer. The film teems with epithets for the informer – 'rat', 'stoolie', 'cheese-eater' – all of them hurled at the film's protagonist, Terry Malloy (Brando), like stones at Saint Stephen. Malloy is presented as an honest man who just wants to do his job. He shies away from confronting the truth about his union, that it is dominated by racketeers who are controlling and, in some cases, destroying the lives of his colleagues. But the corruption touches him from the very beginning of the story when he is unwittingly involved in luring a workmate to his death ('I thought they were just going to lean on him a little', says Terry after a couple of mob henchmen have hurled his friend Joey from a rooftop). We soon learn that the dead man was about to give evidence against Johnny Friendly whose right-hand man, Charley the Gent (Rod Steiger) is Terry's older brother. The local priest (Karl Malden) is sickened by this latest example of mob violence and

Kazan (on right) directs Brando in this rooftop scene from On the Waterfront. *In the background, wearing hat and glasses, is the film's director of photography, Boris Kaufman.*

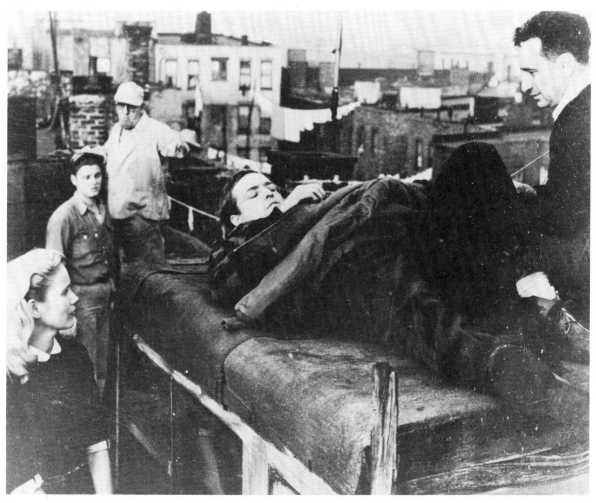

calls a meeting of longshoremen at his church where he is accompanied by the dead man's sister, Edie (Eva Marie Saint). At this point, too, the Waterfront Crime Commission moves in to investigate mob control and to clean up the waterfront. Terry refuses to talk to them – he has no intention of becoming an informer. It is only after he has fallen in love with Edie that he wavers in his intent. When the mob murders Charley as a warning to him, Terry finally goes before the Commission to testify against Friendly. He is beaten up, goes back on the waterfront but leads his comrades back to work.

Kazan's allegory is clear. The mob represents the communists that Kazan believed were controlling the entertainment industry; the Crime Commission stands in for HUAC; the priest – based on a real person – is used symbolically as the voice of Terry's conscience. Terry Malloy is, of course, Elia Kazan, defying the disapproval of his colleagues to be true to his principles – except Terry Malloy is not motivated by principle. He is moved to act by guilt (over his involvement in Joey's death); desire (for the love of Joey's sister); revenge (for the death of his own brother) and, finally, pride (shown in his insistence that he is seen to be somebody instead of 'just a bum').

The plot falls apart almost entirely with the death of Charley Malloy – there is no logic in his murder, it serves no purpose except as a plotting device to drive Terry out of his silence and into the arms of the Crime Commission. Terry's final confrontation with Johnny Friendly comes after Friendly has been totally discredited; it is presented as an old-fashioned 'showdown' between the Good Guy and the Bad Guy. Terry's workmates stand around like sheep, ready to follow the stronger man. This aspect of the film led several contemporary commentators to question the film's morality. In a 1955 *Sight and Sound* article which concentrated solely on the film's last sequence, Lindsay Anderson argued that the film's conclusion is unambiguously 'fascist'. It is also, he states plainly, 'a bad film'. Anderson is right. The film is fraudulent, manipulative and meritricious. But it also happens to contain Marlon Brando's finest, and most influential, screen performance.

As Terry Malloy, Brando made full use of the naturalistic detail he had displayed in his stage portrayals of Sage McRae and Stanley Kowalski. His eyes are continuously on the move, searching out the truth in others or else reflecting his own inner confusion; his hands fill the gaps when words fail him; his body constantly shrugs as if to rid itself of some invisible burden. He smiles a great deal, sometimes defensively but always with a touching openness – even the brief flashes of machismo, as when Terry outlines his 'philosophy of life' ('do it to him before he does it to you'), are more poignant than threatening.

Brando appears not to be acting at all, but merely behaving – but it

Terry and Edie's first encounter (below) and later, in the park (bottom).

The love scenes between Terry (Brando) and Edie (Eva Marie Saint) are beautifully played and remain the most satisfying parts of the film.

is a performance, tirelessly sustained. It is a peak of screen naturalism and, like all great cinema performances, the keynote is one of intimacy. It brings together elements of Brando's earlier film roles: the self-examination of Ken Wilocek; the anger of Kowalski; the martyrdom of Zapata; the righteousness of Antony; the posturing allure of Johnny – all blended together into a seemingly complete portrait of a tormented man. All of Brando's appeal, and much of his significance for other actors, can be found in his portrayal of Terry Malloy. His faults are here, too, as when he fails to edit the performance in scenes where physical economy might have been less distracting – even if it may have felt less realistic. Kazan indulges Brando, covering this flaw by favouring him in many of the camera set-ups. This is the Brando that other actors imitate, and future attempts at naturalism would reveal the mannered fussiness of 'method' improvisation.

There is a famous scene in the film where Terry and Edie are shown walking in a park. She drops her glove and he picks it up but, instead of offering it back to her, he puts it on his own hand and continues the conversation – prolongs it rather – by keeping the glove back from her. It is well known that Eva Marie Saint dropped the glove accidentally and that Brando improvised the little game Terry plays with it. The scene works well and progresses nicely until it reaches the rehearsed section where Terry pulls out a stick of chewing gum and offers it to Edie. Now the scene seems overloaded with business.

That Brando knows the virtue of stillness is demonstrated in an earlier scene when Charley comes to ask his brother to keep an eye on the local priest. Here, Brando sits quite still while a crouched Rod Steiger springs on the balls of his feet, snatches at the pages of a magazine and overloads the scene with unnecessary detail. Steiger is working hard, but the audience is watching Brando.

The most frequently anthologised scene from the film is the one set in the back of a taxi-cab where Charley makes a last attempt to dissuade Terry from testifying. Once again, Kazan's camera angles are designed to favour Brando and, at one point, Steiger can be seen opening his mouth to speak – only to have Kazan cut to Brando's close-up before the words can come out. The scene is chiefly remembered for Brando's 'I could have been a contender' speech, which is nicely written and well-delivered but placed in a wholly artificial context. Steiger is required to set it up for Brando by dealing with an awkward shift into vague reminiscence. The appeal of this scene lies with the sentiments expressed by Brando's character, sentiments which touch chords in many people who would like to have amounted to something in their lives. It is a showy scene – an actor's scene (Brando's, that is, since Steiger is ill-served), but the power of Brando's performance is not best observed here, nor in his slow, masochistic walk at the end of the film.

The most anthologised scene from On the Waterfront *and the source of a million Brando imitations: Charley Malloy (Rod Steiger) pulls a gun on his brother Terry and cues one of the most famous speeches in the movies.*

The scenes between Brando and Eva Marie Saint are the best in the film. Here, Brando shades in all the areas of Terry's character: his fear, his pride, his confusion. The dialogue is often standard romantic banter, descending to banality on occasion, but Brando and Saint transcend the words and play the situation of two young people in the throes of a troubled love affair. Kazan's camera is no more favourable to Saint than it is to Steiger, but, unlike Steiger, Saint does not attempt to compete with Brando. She complements him, and her performance is better for it. Brando responds to her technique, picking up the emotional cues she gives out in much the same way that he picked up her dropped glove. When Edie strokes Terry's cheek during their first date in a bar, his face registers his shyness at this unaccustomed tenderness, but his expression changes slightly to reveal something deeper – his inner shame over Joey's death.

The Waterfront priest, Father Barry (Karl Malden at far left), warns Terry's co-workers to leave him alone as he staggers up the ramp to work after being beaten up by Johnny Friendly's 'heavies'.

Clearly, the camera is in collusion with Brando throughout the film as Kazan focusses our attention on Terry's reaction to events around him. The intensity of Brando's concentration produces the powerful effect of the actor as emotional seismograph, drawing us ever more deeply into identification with his character's dilemma.

The camera was not the only aspect of the film that was made subservient to Brando's performance. Leonard Bernstein, who wrote the plangent musical score for the film, recalled the anxiety of dubbing that score with Kazan: 'There is a tender, hesitant love scene on the roof between the inarticulate hero and the inhibited heroine, surrounded by cooing pigeons. It was deliberately underwritten, and there are long, Kazan-like pauses between the lines – an ideal spot, it would seem, for the composer to take over. I suggested that here I should write love music that was shy at first and then, with growing *Tristanesque* intensity, comes to a great climax which swamps the scene and screen, even drowning out the last prosaic bits of dialogue, which went something like this: "Have a beer with me?" (Very long pause) "Uh-uh". The music here was to do the real storytelling and Kazan and company agreed enthusiastically, deciding to do it this way before even one note was written. So it was written, orchestrated and recorded. But then (in the dubbing studio) Kazan decided he just couldn't give up that ineffably sacred grunt which Brando emits at the end – it was, he thought, perhaps the two most eloquent syllables the actor had delivered in the whole script. And what happened to the music? As it mounts to its great climax as the theme goes higher and higher and brasses and percussion join in with the strings and woodwinds, the all-powerful control dials are turned and the sound fades out in a slow *diminuendo*. Musically ridiculous, of course, and to save a grunt...'

Alongside Bernstein's music, there are other things to admire in *On the Waterfront*: the fine black and white cinematography of Boris Kaufman (who had made his reputation as Jean Vigo's cameraman); the playing of Eva Marie Saint – but it is unquestionably Marlon Brando's extraordinary performance which ensured that the film would appear to be something more than an apologia by Kazan and Schulberg for their behaviour. Few American critics commented on the political sub-text; the film was welcomed by them, and received by the public, as a morality tale about a simple man coming to terms with his conscience or else as a kind of urban *High Noon* (ironic, in view of Carl Foreman's fate). Writing in 1972, the critic Colin MacArthur saw *On The Waterfront* as a film whose themes were 'common in the gangster films of the late Thirties'. From this standpoint, MacArthur argues that 'it is part of the character of Terry Malloy that he is not fully aware of the complexity of his motives' and that 'the traditions of denouement within the gangster genre are individualistic'. The New

York critics gave it their award as Best Film of 1954, and Brando was named Best Actor.

The critical acclaim was reflected in the Academy Awards that were lavished on the film: Best Picture; Best Director (Kazan); Best Story and Screenplay (Schulberg); Best Cinematography (Kaufman); Best Art Direction (Richard Day); Best Editing (Gene Milford); Best Actress (Saint) and Best Actor (Brando). Brando had finally won his Oscar and, although he claimed to have disliked the film when he first saw it, he received the accolade with grace and modesty. After commenting that the Oscar was 'much heavier than I imagined', Brando told the Academy Award audience 'I don't think that ever in my life have so many people been so directly responsible for my being so very, very glad. It's a wonderful moment and a rare one and I am certainly indebted. Thank you.'

The Oscar was a signal of Hollywood approval for Brando – he had beaten off competition from such well-loved veterans as Humphrey Bogart and Bing Crosby. Brando was no longer viewed as an outsider or an upstart. He had six decent film performances behind him and no-one could deny that he was now a major star.

Elia Kazan has spoken of the sense of power he felt after the success of *On the Waterfront*. He knew that he now had the freedom to work with whomsoever he liked on whatever he liked. The film seemed to have brought the same power to Brando. Of course, power for an actor is not the same thing as power for a director. More often than not, it removes them from the area where they could do their best work, giving them the capacity to earn more money rather than to stretch their talents. As Terry Malloy, Brando had shown himself to be an actor to be measured against the best on the screen, but the quality of an actor's performance has never been of enduring value in Hollywood.

Brando took time to adjust to his newly elevated status. He disliked *On The Waterfront* when he first saw it some months before its premiere at the Venice Film Festival. As for the Academy Award, he would not receive this until he had completed his next film and was mid-way through another. On the personal front, he was concerned about his mother's health. Dorothy Brando had developed kidney and liver problems which were giving cause for serious concern. Kazan did manage to convince Brando that his work on *Waterfront* had been worthwhile but the actor seemed more interested in pursuing possibilities in Europe.

There was certainly no shortage of interesting offers and Brando became partially committed to several projects including a French language version of *Lady Chatterley's Lover* for director Marc Allegret, and an adaptation of Stendhal's *The Red and the Black* for the veteran Claude Autant-Lara. On this last project, he was replaced by Gérard Philipe, Brando's more romantic opposite number in France. Many of

Grace Kelly (winner of the 1954 Best Actress Oscar) receives a congratulatory kiss from Brando, who was named Best Actor for his performance in Waterfront.

69

the problems with the European projects were financial, as was the case with Luchino Visconti's *Senso* – the director wanted Brando and Ingrid Bergman, but financial constraints dictated that he cast Farley Granger and Alida Valli. These European setbacks notwithstanding, any actor with an eye on his career would have been careful in his next choice of job. Unfortunately, just as he had followed *Julius Caesar* with *The Wild One*, so Brando would follow *On the Waterfront* with a film that would go beyond disappointment and lead many to believe him to have an aberrant nature.

It may have been purely for the money on offer, but his decision to sign with Twentieth-Century Fox for a costume drama called *The Egyptian* seemed unusually perverse when his career was so securely in the ascendant. The film's director was to be Michael Curtiz, a Hungarian with a reputation for turning out routine films with exceptional speed. Along the way, Curtiz had directed such films as *Casablanca*, *The Sea Hawk* and *The Adventures of Robin Hood*, but these must be set against scores of lesser works, and he did appear to be an odd choice of director to follow Kazan.

Brando as a sullen Napoleon Bonaparte in Desirée, *his first film in colour. His appearance in the film was by way of paying a contractual debt to Twentieth Century Fox, and Brando, recovering from the recent death of his mother, gave a lacklustre performance.*

The supporting cast was no more inspiring: Victor Mature and Bella Darvi. Darvi, who would be making her screen debut, was actually Darryl Zanuck's mistress and her exotic-sounding surname was simply a combination of Zanuck's first name and that of his wife, Virginia (an indelicate move on his part). As for Mature, he was an actor who had chosen the easier role of film star: he had once been refused membership to a California country club on the grounds that he was an actor. 'I'm no actor,' he complained, 'And I've got twenty pictures to prove it.' The partnership of this self-mocking lightweight with an actor of Brando's talent did not appear incongruous to Zanuck. To Brando, however, it did. In addition, the final script bore little resemblance to the original draft he had read and approved. As shooting was about to begin, Dorothy Brando's health went into a rapid decline, causing Brando deep distress, and, at the last moment, he walked off the picture, leaving Zanuck without a leading man but unable to cancel the production.

Zanuck and Fox sued Brando for $2 million and the only way the actor could ameliorate the situation was by agreeing to appear in another Fox production by way of compensation. Edmund Purdom replaced Brando in *The Egyptian*, which in the end was not much worse than *Desiree*, the film Brando found himself forced to star in. But before that, in March 1954, Dorothy Brando died and Brando attended the funeral with his father, sisters and aunt Bette. Shortly afterwards, he told friends that he was greatly impressed by his mother's courage in the face of death. The pain caused by his bereavement may account in part for the somnambulistic performance Brando gave in this next film.

In following his performance as Terry Malloy with his portrayal of Napoleon Bonaparte in *Desirée*, (with Jean Simmons as Desirée) Brando slipped from the sublime to the ridiculous. He has called it 'the most shaming performance of my life', but it is barely a performance at all. There is no indication here that this is an actor of talent, let alone one of exceptional quality.

According to the late Sammy Davis Jr., Brando indulged his fondness for mimicry by giving his Napoleon the silky voice of British actor, Claude Rains (best remembered today as the sympathetic police chief in *Casablanca*). Rains as Napoleon would have been something to see, but Brando was a disappointment. The film's German-born director was Henry Koster, a charming and courteous man who had made his name with a series of vehicles for the singing star Deanna Durbin. Koster, whose father was an avid collector of Napoleonic memorabilia, recalled that Brando had no notion of how to play the French emperor, and there were many loud disagreements on the set. Off-camera, however, Brando and Koster struck up a warm friendship and the director found his star a very likeable man whose kindness and loyalty to his friends were quite remarkable. Brando arranged for several of his friends – many of whom had been on the *Arms and the Man* tour – to be engaged in the film's cast or crew. One of these was Philip Rhodes who had now become a fixture as Brando's personal make-up man. Brando got along well, too, with Jean Simmons but his lack of interest is evident throughout the film, which retains only the curiosity value of containing the actor's first appearance in colour.

Brando with fellow Universal Studio star, Marilyn Monroe.

His debt to Fox paid, Brando was resolved to be more cautious in future. But still this did not lead him to accept the most obvious choice of role. In 1952, Sam Goldwyn had had a big success with a Frank Loesser musical, *Hans Christian Andersen*, which had been conceived as a vehicle for the Goldwyn star, Danny Kaye. This prompted Goldwyn to buy the film rights to Loesser's stage hit, *Guys and Dolls*; this time he had Gene Kelly in mind to play Sky Masterson, the charming, compulsive gambler, in the musical based on Damon Runyon's comic short stories. The musical had been an enormous success, having clocked up 1,200 performances on Broadway, and it was considered a very valuable property. But then Goldwyn made two curious decisions. First of all, he signed Joseph L. Mankiewicz to direct, and secondly, when Kelly could not be released from MGM, who had him under contract, Goldwyn offered the lead to Brando. Brando objected that he had never played in a musical before, and received a telegram from Mankiewicz in reply: 'UNDERSTAND YOU'RE APPREHENSIVE BECAUSE YOU'VE NEVER DONE MUSICAL COMEDY. YOU HAVE NOTHING REPEAT NOTHING TO WORRY ABOUT. BECAUSE NEITHER HAVE I. LOVE, JOE.'

Mankiewicz brought in two stars from the original Broadway

'Luck be a Lady' —
Brando needed more than
Lady Luck to get him
through Guys and Dolls
production numbers, and
his singing was 'technically
enhanced' by selective
editing. Here he is with
Stubby Kaye (in light
jacket on the left) and a
visibly wincing Frank
Sinatra at lower right.

Sky Masterson (Brando)
bets Nathan Detroit
(Sinatra) that he cannot
remember the pattern of
his bow-tie in Guys and
Dolls.

production of *Guys and Dolls*, Vivian Blaine as Miss Adelaide and Stubby Kaye as Nicely-Nicely Johnson. Jean Simmons, having endured the rigours of *Desiree* with Brando, was cast as Sarah Brown, the Salvation Army sergeant who becomes the object of Sky Masterson's affections (Goldwyn tried – and failed – to get Grace Kelly), while for the role of Nathan Detroit, played on stage by the Jewish character comedian Sam Levene, Mankiewicz signed Frank Sinatra.

Sinatra as Detroit was as wild a piece of casting as Brando playing Masterson. Mankiewicz was not trying to be adventurous by casting against type. Sinatra was determined to get into the film (although he hoped to play Sky Masterson) and eventually persuaded Mankiewicz to let him play Detroit. Mankiewicz was unhappy at the thought of taking a singer like Sinatra – then at the top of his form – and throwing him away on a character support when he was so clearly well-suited to the leading role, but Mankiewicz was up against Goldwyn – and Goldwyn was set on Brando.

For his part, Brando had confidence in Mankiewicz – they had worked happily together on *Julius Caesar*, after all. Furthermore, he could take some comfort from the fact that Sky Masterson was played on Broadway by Robert Alda, who was also an actor rather than a singer. In any case, he had been assured that his singing would be dubbed by a professional.

When it came to it, Brando was given singing lessons and a voice test – largely because it was proving difficult to find a singer to match his high-pitched speaking voice. Frank Loesser's verdict, that Brando had 'a pleasing, husky baritone' put an end to all thought of dubbing and the publicity office had the best advertising catch-line since 'GARBO LAUGHS!' – 'BRANDO SINGS!'

Mankiewicz had built a reputation on his confidence with actors and his ability to write 'great dialogue' with the result that films like *All About Eve*, *People Will Talk* and *The Barefoot Contessa* were remembered as much for the sharp lines they contained as for their star performances by Bette Davis, Cary Grant and Humphrey Bogart. He could always be relied upon to 'pep up' a sparse script with one-liners and additional scenes which, while it had worked to his advantage in the past, was exactly wrong for the book of Loesser's musical. Jo Swerling and Abe Burrows had written a book which kept the chat down to a minimum and moved the plot along neatly without getting in the way of the songs. Mankiewicz, on the other hand, was inclined to write in scenes which gave more of a flavour of Runyon but made the script much too wordy. He was not helped by Sinatra who wanted the part of Nathan Detroit – something of a comic foil to Sky Masterson originally – built up to balance him with Brando.

Brando entered the world of musical comedy completely unarmed

– that is to say he could neither sing nor play comedy. He saw *Guys and Dolls* as a way of extending himself but he was severely hampered by the fact that, while he was singing the lead role, one of the men backing him was Frank Sinatra. Furthermore, Sinatra refused to sing his role, as written, with a heavy Bronx accent. This infuriated Brando who asked Mankiewicz to speak to Sinatra about it. Mankiewicz however felt ill-disposed to tell Frank Sinatra how to sing. Matters worsened when Brando received his *On The Waterfront* Oscar during the filming. Sinatra was equally competitive as an actor – especially since winning his Oscar for *From Here To Eternity* – and he was still smarting from losing the role of Terry Malloy – a Hoboken boy like himself – to Brando – a mid-Westerner. He was determined to make an impact in their scenes together but was frustrated by Brando's slower working methods. Sinatra had a tendency to hit his stride quickly, often giving his best performance in the first take. Brando's frequent requests for re-takes led Sinatra to complain to Mankiewicz, 'Don't put me in the game, coach, until Mumbles has finished rehearsing.'

The final ignominy for Sinatra must have come in the 'Luck Be A Lady' number when he found himself stuck in the chorus backing a Sky Masterson who could not carry a tune four steps without dropping it. For his part, Brando found his co-star's complaints petty. He had initially been pleased to meet Sinatra but now he dismissed him with a remark worthy of Runyon himself: 'Sinatra', said Brando, 'is the kind of guy who, when he dies, is going to go up to heaven and give God a bad time for making him bald.'

A stiff-looking Brando is choreographed by a patient Michael Kidd during rehearsals for Guys and Dolls.

Problems with Sinatra apart, Brando had difficulty in catching the comedy of the role. His approach to a comic line was to draw a huge circle around it. As the great tragedian Edmund Kean observed on his death-bed: 'Dying is easy – *comedy* is difficult.'

Nobody came out of *Guys and Dolls* with very much credit, with the exception of Stubby Kaye and Vivian Blaine, who seemed to have wandered in from another, better movie. Mankiewicz laid many of the problems at Goldwyn's door for insisting on shooting the film in the Cinemascope format, but the stylised settings were Mankiewicz's own idea, and might have worked well in the hands of a Minnelli or Stanley Donen. Most critics admired the charm of Jean Simmons' performance and were kind about Brando – although, the *New Yorker* noted that he sang 'through a rather unyielding set of sinuses'. He is not actually bad, just inadequate. His poor singing is disguised by clever sound engineering; his dancing is self-conscious but you feel he is doing his best. In short, in playing Sky Masterson – a man who will do almost anything for a bet – Brando's identification with his character's philosophy appears total.

Brando knew that *Guys and Dolls* would not mark the change of

Brando relaxes between takes on the set of Guys and Dolls.

pace he was looking for. It seemed only to demonstrate how much he was out of his depth in anything but the serious drama that had made his name. Like any actor, he was keen to test himself, to extend his range. But he was difficult to cast. As *The Times* observed of his performance as Sky Masterson: 'Mr. Brando does very nicely as a musical-comedy hero, but then...he should never do anything very nicely. He is a tiger as an actor and he should behave as a tiger.' The trouble was that there were very few parts for tigers in Hollywood in 1954, and Brando had already conquered that territory. His versatility had not been properly tested, and he was determined to show it, even if that meant fully embracing his position as a film star.

5

Marlon of the movies

An early promotional shot of Brando in archetypal movie-star pose (above). Guys and Dolls *gave studio publicists their best catch-line since 'Garbo laughs!' — 'Brando sings!'*

FOR ALL its shortcomings, *Guys and Dolls* performed well at the box office and confirmed Brando's status as a major star capable of attracting a large audience. His best work may have been in *On the Waterfront* but the musical made more money – for that matter, *Desirée* made more money. The studios could not have been more pleased with Brando and he, for his part, seemed to be coming to terms with the Hollywood way.

A return to the theatre or a move to Europe, both of which were real options, seemed less appropriate to Brando at this time. He had found his *métier* as an actor on film and was not keen to endure the boredom of the lengthy rehearsals and long runs of stage work. As for Europe, he appeared to view that as a retreat. He was in a position to encourage American cinema to tackle important topics in the way that European films had done. There was a spirit of compromise and optimism evident in the Brando of 1955. He excused the excesses of Hollywood movies: 'We've been too busy building a continent,' he said, 'But I think we'll catch up in the end.' This was no rebel talking, this was a mature young actor who was preparing to invest his considerable talent in his native film industry. It was to prove a costly experiment.

After the release of *Guys and Dolls* Brando set up his own production company, Pennebaker Productions (named in memory of his mother). Pennebaker received backing from Paramount Pictures and, while Brando claimed he intended it to spearhead his commitment to American film he was also using it to provide financial security for his father. Marlon Brando Snr. was made a director of Pennebaker Productions, in company with two press agents – George Glass, who had been one of Stanley Kramer's associates, and Walter Seltzer. The board was completed by George Englund, a young man with ambitions

PICTURE
POST

December 3, 1955

MARLON
BRANDO
SINGS!

4^D

WEEK ENDING
3 DECEMBER 1955

THE PERSECUTION OF JULES DASSIN
AN EX-GANGSTER THROWS A PARTY
WILL TV KILL THE BRITISH SUNDAY?

HULTON'S
NATIONAL
WEEKLY

EVERY
WEDNESDAY

77

to become a producer-director. These four directors were instructed to scout suitable projects but Brando himself showed little interest in the company and his next venture came via MGM.

Teahouse of the August Moon, by John Patrick (from a novel by Vern Scheider) had been a hit play on Broadway, and its theme – the culture clash between American servicemen and the post-war Japanese they are meant to be rehabilitating – appealed to Brando. He had seen the play several times and particularly admired the performance of David Wayne as Sakini, the Okinawan interpreter assigned to the American Captain Fisby (played on stage by John Forsythe). Wayne had appeared in films, sometimes memorably (he was the songwriter who lived next door to Spencer Tracy and Katherine Hepburn in *Adam's Rib*) but he was not considered a star. Nevertheless, it seemed likely that he would be invited to re-create his stage role for the film of *Teahouse*. MGM's Head of Production, Dore Schary, had more or less decided on Gene Kelly for Fisby with David Wayne as Sakini when Brando expressed an interest in the project. He was immediately offered the role of Fisby – effectively, the lead. But Brando saw much more opportunity for himself in the role of the interpreter, and asked to be considered for this instead. Schary agreed and, such was Brando's newly acquired eminence, he actually allowed the actor to approve the director and screenwriter.

Brando's choice of director was Daniel Mann (whose credits included *Come Back, Little Sheba* and *I'll Cry Tomorrow*) and he insisted that John Patrick should write the screenplay. With Brando as Sakini, Schary brought in Glenn Ford as Fisby and Louis Calhern to play the important supporting role of Fisby's commanding officer, Colonel Purdy. Brando had warmed to Calhern during the shooting of *Julius Caesar* and was pleased to be working with him again. As a project then, *Teahouse of the August Moon* satisfied many of the criteria Brando was using to measure his film work. It offered a chance for him to prove his ability to play character comedy, and it addressed itself to a serious subject in an entertaining and accessible way. Furthermore, it would be filmed on location in Japan. The first disappointment came with the location. Brando arrived in Tokyo on 23rd April, 1956. He had been touring South-East Asia scouting locations for a vaguely conceived documentary which he hoped to make under the Pennebaker banner about the problems of the hungry and the underprivileged in that part of the world. After meeting with the rest of the MGM unit in Tokyo, Brando joined them on the trip to the *Teahouse* location at Nara. Unfortunately, Nara was in the grip of persistent rain and the effective working days were few and far between.

Brando established a good rapport with John Patrick but soon found himself at odds with both Glenn Ford and Daniel Mann. Ford had the larger role but was being paid considerably less than Brando.

Naturally, a certain resentment grew and this was exacerbated by the differing approaches of the actors. Brando had spent a great deal of time preparing for his performance as Sakini – he studied Japanese and worked long and hard to perfect the Okinawan accent in English. He often took time to work his way into a scene. Like Sinatra on *Guys and Dolls*, Ford was inclined to work quickly and was often past his best when Brando was sufficiently 'warmed up'.

Mann was having to contend with the bad weather and was under pressure from MGM to return to the studio and continue filming on the back lot, while Brando felt that they should wait it out until the rain passed. After five weeks in Japan, disaster struck the unit when Louis Calhern suffered a heart attack and died. Brando had been very fond of Calhern but he was aware that the older actor was embroiled in an unhappy affair with a much younger woman, and that this was made worse by his heavy drinking. Brando sent a telegram to John Patrick in America: 'Lou died in his sleep last night, and I'm glad. He was so lonely and unhappy that he really didn't want to live.'

The rain continued, and MGM prevailed. The unit moved back to California where Calhern's role was taken over by Paul Ford (who had played the part on Broadway). Ford would go on to repeat his characterisation of the bumbling Colonel in the long-running *Phil Silvers Show* ('Sgt. Bilko') on television.

Teahouse of the August Moon was not destined to be the film Brando had hoped for. His diligence in preparing for the role was appreciated by those in the know who could attest that his Okinawan accent was impeccable. But the majority of film critics, along with the general public, received his Sakini as a portrayal in the time-honoured tradition of the 'wily oriental gentleman'. The film betrays its stage origins from the very beginning when Sakini speaks direct to the camera: 'In Okinawa, no locks on doors. Bad manners not to trust neighbours. In America, lock and key big business. Conclusion – bad manners good business.' This lively soliloquy is well-handled by Brando and serves to introduce his character and set up the situation. His make-up is excellent – he looks convincingly Japanese – but he lacks the lightness of figure and manner that seem necessary for the character.

The major problem, as with *Guys and Dolls*, is one of aptitude. Brando cannot play comedy. It is a serious failing in an actor of his ability. This is not to say that he is without humour; quite the contrary, he can lace a performance with real wit on occasion. But when required to be funny, he simply pulls faces and misjudges lines. His portrayal of Sakini is a perfect example of fine observation subordinated to clumsy technique. Brando is a great tragic actor – but in comedy he is the worst kind of ham. His skill is such that he can convince us that Sakini, not Brando himself, is the ham. But that is

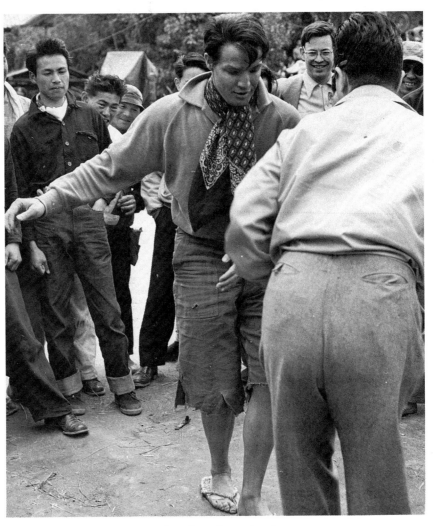

Brando relished the opportunity of mixing with local people that was afforded by overseas location filming. Here, between takes for Teahouse of the August Moon, *Brando joins in a Japanese game.*

only because he has learned to be a ham in character.

For a while Brando busied himself with Pennebaker Productions, considering possible projects and even beginning work on a script (a Western with the unlikely title of *A Burst of Vermilion*). When none of his own projects seemed likely to come to anything, Brando persuaded Warner Brothers to accept Pennebaker as co-producers on a film in which he would appear.

The film was *Sayonara*, and it would give Brando a chance to return to Japan – this time, he believed, with a serious and intelligent story. The idea for the film came from the theatre and film director, Joshua Logan. Logan had worked with the novelist James A. Michener on the adaptation of his book 'Tales of the South Pacific' into the Rodgers and Hammerstein musical *South Pacific*. Passionate about

Japan and its culture, Logan had suggested to Michener that he write a modern version of *Madame Butterfly* centred on the recent American occupation of Japan. Michener liked the idea, which formed the basis of *Sayonara*, his best-selling novel about inter-racial love and he allowed Logan to acquire the screen rights to the book.

Logan had tried to get Brando for one of his earlier projects, the film of his stage success, *Mister Roberts*. Henry Fonda had played the lead role on Broadway but Logan had wanted Brando for the film. When John Ford was hired as director, he dismissed any thought of casting Brando in place of Fonda.

Brando considered Logan to be sympathetic – he knew Logan because he had cast Brando's sister Jocelyn in the only female role in the stage production of *Mister Roberts* some years before. Moreover, the idea of returning to Japan under happier circumstances appealed to Brando. Warners made an offer of $300,000, plus a percentage, plus expenses and Brando signed to make *Sayonara* without having read the script.

In *Sayonara*, Brando plays Major Lloyd Gruver, a veteran of the Korean war posted to Japan to recover from combat fatigue and be near his fiancée, thanks to the influence of her father, General Webster. Here, Gruver acts as best man at the wedding of his colleague Joe Kelly (Red Buttons) to a young Japanese girl. The Air Force, which takes a dim view of miscegenation, takes steps to return Kelly to America without his new wife. By this time, Gruver has abandoned his fiancée and taken up with a Japanese girl himself. Distraught, Kelly and his wife, who is pregnant, commit suicide. Gruver's new girlfriend leaves him, but he persuades her to marry him and the repatriation rules are changed just in time.

Clever make-up made Brando look convincingly Japanese as Sakini in Teahouse.

The story is pure soap opera or, as Brando himself described it, 'wondrous hearts-and-flowers nonsense that was supposed to be a serious picture about Japan'. Logan had expected Brando to want the part of Joe Kelly, the tragic lover but he chose Gruver, observing that it would be 'interesting to play someone who was pompous and superior and square'. The character was written as a Westerner, but Brando elected to make him a Texan which allowed him to confront the race prejudices that were common in the Southern states. The accent was, as always, precisely observed but it revealed another weakness in Brando's work. He has a fondness for accents but, no matter how exactly he places them, they always sound imposed. The distinct Brando tone purrs through under them. He is a gifted mimic, but the mimicry is all too obviously a device – like Olivier's false noses. Some of his performances would be more truthful if he abandoned the carefully adopted accent and just played the emotion of a role. As Terry Malloy, Brando 'coloured' certain phrases but it was otherwise a very generalised New York accent. The very accuracy of an accent often heightens the artificiality of a performance.

The artificiality of Lloyd Gruver cannot however be laid purely at Brando's door. Logan's film is overlong (running close to two and a half hours) and padded out with scenes which would look more comfortable in a travelogue. When Brando complained to Logan about the script by Paul Osborn, the director invited him to re-write sections of it himself. Brando went through the entire screenplay, re-working scene after scene. In doing so, he failed to take into account the need for Warners to have the full co-operation of the Air Force, which meant that the film had to soften its criticism of the official attitude to miscegenation. The other problem with the film's approach was that Logan had originally hoped to produce the story on stage as a musical in the *South Pacific* tradition. The result was Logan retained a sugary conception which jarred with the issues that had attracted Brando to the story.

Logan did not hide his admiration for Brando's talent. 'He is the best actor I've met since Garbo,' he declared, 'a genius.' Brando interpreted this adulation as a sign of directorial weakness and made it clear that he had little confidence in Logan's visualisation of the script. Very few of Brando's emendations were included in the final screenplay and, even where they were, Logan was able to overrule the actor. In the scene where Gruver discovers the bodies of Joe Kelly and his wife, Brando wanted to have an impassioned speech while Logan preferred him to react very quietly with a whispered 'Oh, no.' It was decided to shoot both versions, but Brando's version was never filmed. After playing it Logan's way, he in fact agreed with the director that the quiet understatment was more effective.

One change that Brando managed to keep in the script was the final reconciliation of his character with the Japanese girl he loves (and who was played with very little animation by Miika Taka). At the end of Michener's book, the couple are separated but uncharacteristically Brando wanted a more upbeat, affirmative conclusion. This, of course, makes nonsense of the film's title – although Brando was quick to claim that 'sayonara' could sometimes mean 'hello'.

It was while *Sayonara* was being completed that Brando agreed to a meeting with the novelist and short-story writer, Truman Capote, who wished to profile the actor for a magazine. This encounter was to have a profound effect on Brando's attitude to the media and there is no doubt that Capote took every advantage of his subject to gain his confidence and encourage him to speak openly about his past life and his current working relationships. Although Capote and Brando drank vodka together, it is more likely that Capote let Brando do most of the drinking. The resulting conversation was worked on by Capote for the next year. He claimed that he chose Brando's name at random and simply wanted to write a profile of a film star – something

*In Japan again for
Sayonara. Local flower
girls greet (left to right)
the director, Joshua
Logan, Brando (in
costume as Lloyd Gruver)
and author James A.
Michener.*

that would usually be full of banalities – and turn it into a 'work
of art'. The piece appeared in the *New Yorker* under the title 'The
Duke in his Domain', and Capote preserved a series of professionally
embarrassing and personally revealing comments from an actor who
was clearly drunk and unhappy. It was a piece of 'below the belt'
journalism with quotes that would not have been out of place in the
tabloids; encased in Capote's semi-precious prose, the article obtained
a veneer of respectability.

When Brando realised that he had, in effect, been tricked by Capote
he wrote a long letter asking to have all references to friends and
colleagues deleted. Capote did not reply to the letter, nor did he

comply with Brando's wishes. He had his copy and he knew it would attract readers. Writing some years later about Brando's reaction to the piece, Capote remarked: 'Though not claiming any inaccuracy, he apparently felt it was an unsympathetic, even treacherous intrusion upon the secret terrain of a suffering and intellectually awesome sensibility. My opinion? Just that it is a pretty good account, and a sympathetic one, of a wounded young man who is a genius, but not markedly intelligent.'

The article appeared in October, 1957, just at the time of Brando's marriage to a young starlet called Anna Kashfi. Brando had met Kashfi in 1955 when she was at Paramount appearing in *The Mountain* opposite Spencer Tracy and Robert Wagner. Their relationship was stormy at the best of times and their marriage was undertaken to legitimise the baby Kashfi was expecting.

The studio publicity handout on Anna Kashfi stated that she had been born in Calcutta in 1934, the daughter of an architect and civil engineer named Devi Kashfi and his wife, Selma Ghose. 'Like every Indian girl,' it went on, 'she learned the classical dances of Asia, and it was while appearing in a class recital that she drew the attention of directors of an Indian motion picture company.' This, as Brando would discover only after his marriage to her, was sheer nonsense.

'Anna Kashfi' was in reality Joanna O'Callaghan from Cardiff. She had indeed been born in Calcutta – her father William Patrick O'Callaghan had been working for the Indian State Railways at the time – but her family had moved to South Wales and settled in Cardiff when Joanna was thirteen. After working as a waitress and cashier in Cardiff, she moved to London and obtained work as a model.

Joanna O'Callaghan's deception recalled Brando's early claims to have been born in Rangoon or Calcutta but, whereas Brando was teasing the public, 'Anna Kashfi' was determined to keep to her fantasy. Her parents in Cardiff were, understandably, distressed and could not understand why she had disowned them. In *Brando for Breakfast*, her autobiographical memoir of her marriage to Brando – which lasted less than a year – she holds fast to the claim that she is Indian, claiming that the O'Callaghans merely adopted her. This unhappy episode might have been put down to bitter experience by Brando had it not been for the birth, in May 1958, of his and Kashfi's son. Brando wanted to name the boy Christian after his friend, the French actor Christian Marquand. Kashfi disapproved of Marquand, claiming that he and Brando 'displayed an affection toward each other that far overstepped the usual expressions of friendship'. She wanted to perpetuate her 'father's' name by calling her son Devi (which actually means 'goddess' in Hindi). They compromised and the boy was named Christian Devi – each parent refusing to address him by the other's choice of name. The couple separated in September 1958, but would

A wedding day shot of Brando and Hollywood starlet Anna Kashfi, October 1957. Kashfi's marriage to Brando, which lasted less than a year, was almost as brief as her film career.

Kashfi in a rather provocative pose for the 'nice Indian girl' she claimed to be. The later revelation that she was actually Joanna O'Callaghan from Cardiff would infuriate Brando.

meet again over a long period as they battled through the courts for custody of their son. This long-term instability was to have a profound effect on Christian, with devastating results.

The unhappy experiences of the Capote profile and his marriage to Anna Kashfi were to have their effect on Brando and cause him to distrust all but those closest to him. It would be a long time before he would give a serious interview to any journalist – no matter how respected the magazine in question. Even when he began to do so, he would talk only about his feelings on civil rights issues affecting black and native Americans. His private life would be a closed book.

Brando's strong sense of indignation over matters of race had led him to accept *Sayonara* and it was a related issue that drew him to the screen adaptation of Irwin Shaw's war novel, *The Young Lions*. As part of the deal he had struck with Twentieth-Century Fox over their 1954 law suit against him for abandoning *The Egyptian*, he agreed to make one more film for them. He accepted *The Young Lions* partly to satisfy that commitment, but also because he saw an opportunity to present a view of a German soldier that would defy the Hollywood stereotype of the day.

Like *Sayonara*, the film was based on a best-seller. Irwin Shaw's novel was set during the Second World War and showed the conflict through the eyes of three ordinary soldiers, two Americans and one German. Twentieth-Century Fox had originally planned to film that story using its own contract players for the lead roles but, when Edward Dmytryk signed on as director, the project was quickly up-graded. Dmytryk had recently directed *Raintree County* for MGM. The stars of this ill-fated attempt to recapture the lost glory of *Gone With The Wind* were Elizabeth Taylor and Brando's former rival, Montgomery Clift. Dmytryk proposed Clift for the role of Noah Ackerman, the young Jewish American who finds it hard to adjust to army life in *The Young Lions*.

Clift was still considered a major star but his career was already edging into decline. He had joined Burt Lancaster and Frank Sinatra in Fred Zinnemann's *From Here to Eternity*, and his performance as the sensitive Private Prewitt had been highly praised, but the actor's personal life was turning into a mess. Unable to come to terms with his homosexuality, Clift had become ever more dependant upon drugs and alcohol. By the time he made *Raintree County* in 1957, Clift had been away from the screen for four years and serious financial difficulties had been added to his private troubles. These soon began to spill over into his work, no more dramatically than with a near-fatal car crash that left his face scarred and partially paralysed. Shooting on *Raintree County* was suspended for several months while Clift was nursed back to health. Friends tried vainly to dissuade him from going back in front of the cameras, but he was determined to honour his commitment to the film. *Raintree County* was an expensive flop but Clift was at least able to prove that his accident had not halted his career. When Dmytryk offered him the role of Ackerman, Clift saw it as a challenge and a way to re-establish himself after the unhappy experience of their earlier film together.

The man who negotiated Clift's contract for *The Young Lions* was Jay Kanter who also represented Brando at MCA. Knowing that Brando had an outstanding debt to Fox, Kanter decided to offer Brando and Clift to the studio as a package. To complete the deal he suggested another of his clients, Dean Martin, for the remaining lead. Martin had recently broken – somewhat acrimoniously – with his screen partner, Jerry Lewis, and he needed a successful role to establish himself in a solo career. With Brando and Clift in the cast, Fox were happy to have their contract artist Tony Randall as the co-star, but Kanter was adamant: if the studio said no to Martin, it could say goodbye to Brando and Clift.

When Martin joined the cast his role as a hard-drinking writer was re-written, making him instead a Broadway entertainer. This was a small change in comparison to the metamorphosis undergone by Brando's character. Instead of Shaw's brutal Nazi sergeant, Brando insisted on playing Christian Diestl as a sensitive man who does not truly understand the evils of Nazism until it is too late. At a press conference for the film in Berlin, he made his intentions clear: 'The picture will show that Nazism is a matter of mind, not geography, that there are Nazis, and people of good will, in every country. The world can't spend its life looking over its shoulder and nursing hatreds. There would be no progress that way.'

Brando with his 'rival' Montgomery Clift on the set of From Here To Eternity, *with the film's director Fred Zinnemann (centre).*

6

A star experiments

B Y 1957, the youthful rivalry between Marlon Brando and Montgomery Clift had been diffused as each one established his own career. Their professional paths had not yet crossed but they often came close to running parallel. Clift had made his film debut in Fred Zinnemann's *The Search* only a short while before Brando debuted with the same director in *The Men*. Just as Clift had taken over Brando's role in *Stazione Termini*, so Brando had stepped in when Clift wisely declined to play Napoleon in *Desirée*. They were not friends, but they clearly respected each other and the notion of them appearing in the same film certainly excited audience expectations.

Brando had already shown his concern about the problems in Clift's private life. During the studio filming of *Teahouse of the August Moon*, he had gone to visit Clift and urged him to take more care of himself. In her excellent biography of Clift, Patricia Bosworth reveals that Clift relayed the gist of Brando's remarks to his friend, Jack Larson. She quotes Larson as saying that Brando seemed pre-occupied with 'the healthy competition that should exist between actors – that existed, say, between a Laurence Olivier and a John Gielgud, between a Richard Burton, then, and a Paul Scofield. These men challenged each other, he said. Now, didn't Monty know that the only actor in America who interested Brando was Monty? Didn't he realise that they had always challenged each other, maddened each other, intrigued each other, ever since they started their careers?'

According to Larson, Brando then told Clift that he had gone to see *A Place in the Sun* (for which Clift received an Oscar nomination alongside Brando's for *Streetcar*) 'hoping that you wouldn't be as good as you were supposed to be, *but you were even better*, and I thought,

Brando as Rio in One-Eyed Jacks. *He undertook the hazardous task of directing this film in which he also played the leading role.*

hell, Monty should get that award.' An astonished Clift claimed to have felt the same thing about Brando's performance as Kowalski, to which Brando replied: 'In a way I hate you, I've always hated you because I want to be better than you, but you're better than me – you're my touchstone, my challenge, and I want you and me to go on challenging each other...and I thought you would until you started this foolishness...'

In *The Young Lions* Brando's Diestl is first introduced as a charming ski-instructor in pre-war Bavaria. His pupil is Margaret, a young American woman (Barbara Rush) who accepts his invitation to a New Year's party. At the party, Margaret is surprised at Diestl's apparent sympathy to Nazism, but he explains that the Nazis 'stand for something hopeful in Germany' and tells her how difficult it is to 'rise above class in Europe'. But he stresses that he is not himself a Nazi, in fact he is not even political. Diestl flirts with Margaret and she enjoys it but tells him that she is about to return to New York and to her fiancé, Michael Whiteacre (Dean Martin).

The action now switches to Occupied France where Diestl has become a lieutenant in the German Army which is approaching Paris. His humane treatment of French civilians is contrasted with the harder approach of his commanding officer Captain Hardenberg (Maximilian Schell). America's entry into the war allows for a meeting between

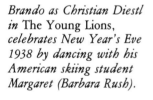

Brando as Christian Diestl in The Young Lions, *celebrates New Year's Eve 1938 by dancing with his American skiing student Margaret (Barbara Rush).*

Whiteacre and Noah Ackerman (Clift) at the Draft Board. Taking pity on his new-found friend, Whiteacre invites Ackerman to a party where he meets, and falls in love with, the decidedly gentile Hope (Hope Lange). Back in Paris, Diestl is attempting to court a young French girl, Francoise (Liliane Montevecchi) who at first sees him as a representative of a murderous occupying army. Diestl is at pains to explain himself: 'I have killed no one,' he tells her, 'but if I had to sacrifice a few lives for peace, I would do it.' Francoise says that 'sacrificing lives for peace' makes no sense to her. Diestl replies: 'I think about this one thousand times a day.' Brando plays this scene with a gentle courtesy that allows Diestl to win Francoise's affection.

Before setting off for Europe, Ackerman marries Hope after overcoming the mild anti-semitism of her father. Whiteacre, on the other hand, decides to postpone his marriage until the end of the war.

The action of the film cuts repeatedly between the American and the German view of the war, with Diestl becoming ever more uncomfortable about his acceptance of the Nazi ideal. When the Normandy invasion sends the Germans into retreat, Diestl – his regiment defeated – stumbles upon a concentration camp and is sickened by its commandant's revelation that he has to kill six thousand prisoners every day. Diestl storms off in disgust, little realising that American troops are just about to enter and liberate the camp. As he wanders through the nearby forest, Diestl hears the approach of two GIs who have themselves just left the concentration camp. As fate would have it, they are none other than Whiteacre and Ackerman. Diestl dashes his rifle against a tree and, as he staggers aimlessly, he is spotted by Whiteacre who – understandably interpreting this as aggression – shoots Diestl dead.

At this point in the film, Brando wanted to have Diestl die with his arms outstretched in symbolic crucifixion or else to have his head come to rest on a coil of barbed wire which would cling to him like a crown of thorns. Clift lodged a strong objection: 'If Marlon does that,' he said, 'I'll walk off the picture.' Brando backed down and Diestl's death scene was considerably less Christ-like.

Nevertheless, the rest of Brando's interpretation was in marked contrast to Irwin Shaw's original conception. The studio accepted the revisions (they wanted Brando for the role) and the screenwriter Ernest Anhalt voiced no objection about incorporating them in the script. On the other hand, Shaw – who had no control over the adaptation of the novel – was totally opposed to this softening of his book's villain. Brando was keen to persuade the author that his changes made for a richer characterisation and there was even talk of the two men debating the point on television.

In the event, Brando might have been better advised to have met

Montgomery Clift, Brando and Dean Martin in costume for the only scene in which they appear together in The Young Lions.

Shaw half-way and portrayed Diestl as an intelligent and cultured man who is irredeemably brutalised by his idealistic Nazism. His belief that the evil was 'a matter of mind, not geography' is given short shrift in the film's American scenes. Granted, Ackerman does encounter a degree of Jew-baiting from his fellow GIs but that is swiftly abandoned when he has distinguished himself under fire. For the most part Brando seems, consciously or unconsciously, to be competing with Clift for the sympathy of the audience.

Clift, his damaged face further transformed by a putty nose and his weight considerably reduced for the role, has an air of fragility that Brando – with his solid physique and dyed blond hair – cannot hope to beat. Even if he had been allowed his 'martyrdom' at the end, Brando's radiant Aryan could not begin to approach the sacrificial quality of Clift's nervous Jew. Diestl dies, but it is Ackerman who seems transfigured by his wartime experience.

In the matter of versatility, however, Brando had again shown his zest for character acting. Once more, he displayed his skill with an accent, lightly flavouring his lines with Germanic expression, and he was able to catch the courtly watchfulness of Diestl as the truth dawns on him. Unfortunately, the decision to promote the character from a lowly sergeant removes any direct comparison with the Americans and Brando's reluctance fully to explore Diestl's darker side makes the performance seem more schematic than the actor might have intended.

If Brando had hoped the *The Young Lions* would have something significant to say about war, he must have been sorely disappointed. It is good of its type, but its type is the old-fashioned Hollywood war picture with a touch of romance 'for the ladies'. That a film could tackle such a subject in a thought-provoking manner was proved by a much more modest film which was released at the same time.

Paths of Glory was set during the First World War and told of a shamefully 'cosmetic' court martial in the French Army. It was distinguished by its direct, unsentimental approach and a clutch of intelligent performances. When Brando found himself looking for a director for his next film – the first fully-fledged effort from Pennebaker Productions – he selected the director of *Paths of Glory*, a young man called Stanley Kubrick.

Pennebaker Productions had become a very expensive sideline for Brando. Much of his money was being swallowed up in the development of various projects for the company. Pennebaker did become involved in a small way in a few films – *Shake Hands With The Devil*, a story of Irish Republicanism starring James Cagney and directed by the British director, Michael Anderson, and Gary Cooper's last film *The Naked Edge*, (again directed by Anderson) but these were hardly major projects. Paramount Pictures had turned down Brando's own script, 'A Burst of Vermilion' but the actor remained strongly interested in

Christian Diestl at the Nazi concentration camp where he finally realises that Hitler's party might not, after all, 'stand for something hopeful in Germany'.

making a western. With this in mind, the independent producer Frank P. Rosenberg passed a script to Brando via MCA. It was an adaptation, by a then little-known television writer called Sam Peckinpah, of Charles Neider's novel, 'The Authentic Death of Hendry Jones' and Rosenberg thought it was ideally suited to Brando.

Brando liked the story-line, but felt the script needed to be totally re-written, so he called in the novelist and screenwriter Calder Willingham to begin revisions. When a new script was ready, Brando was still dissatisfied and he called a lengthy series of script conferences on the film, now called *One-Eyed Jacks* for himself, Willingham and Stanley Kubrick.

It soon became apparent to Kubrick that Brando wanted to exert an enormous amount of control over the finished film, leaving the director with very little freedom. The two men disagreed over the casting of Brando's old friend, Karl Malden (Kubrick wanted Spencer Tracy for the co-starring role of Dad Longworth) and the director finally left the film 'by mutual consent'. Kubrick had found the endless script meetings exhausting but he was full of praise for Brando's ability to improvise scenic development and dialogue and spoke at the time of his regret at having to quit and of his 'respect and admiration for one of the world's foremost artists, Marlon Brando.'

With Paramount backing the film, and most of the roles now cast, Brando was under immense pressure to find a speedy replacement for Kubrick and begin shooting. He decided to direct it himself, and on 2nd December 1958 he assembled his cast and crew in Monterey and set to work.

Aside from Brando and Malden, the cast included Katy Jurado (who had won praise for her performance in *High Noon*), Ben Johnson (a stalwart member of John Ford's 'stock company') and Pina Pellicer, a young Mexican actress whose unhappily neurotic personality led her to commit suicide some time later.

According to the veteran western writer, Frank Gruber, there are seven basic types of western: the railroad story; the ranch story; the Empire story (a grander version of the second category); the revenge story; the Cavalry and Indian story; the outlaw story and, finally the lawman story. It is fair to say that almost every western made at the height of the genre's popularity (which extended from the silent era to the sixties) fits into one or more of Gruber's archetypes. *One-Eyed Jacks* was a revenge story.

Rio (Brando) and Dad Longworth are bank robbers who are pursued into the Mexican desert where one of their horses dies. On the toss of a coin, Dad rides off in search of another horse, promising to return and rescue Rio. He takes with him the proceeds of their latest robbery but, not surprisingly, leaves Rio to be captured and imprisoned. Five years later, Rio is released from prison and tracks down his old partner

Brando, in costume as the bandit Rio, directs One-Eyed Jacks. *His final un-cut version of the film ran to a length of four hours and forty minutes!*

in the town of Monterey where he is now the local sheriff and married to a beautiful Mexican woman (Katy Jurado). Rio rides into town with a small band of outlaws, intent on robbing the bank and revenging himself on Dad. Once there, he falls in love with Jurado's daughter (Pellicer) which delays his plans. Rio pretends to have forgiven Dad's treachery, but the sheriff is suspicious and, when Rio is involved in a gunfight, Dad horsewhips him and runs him out of town. While Rio is recovering, his new partners become impatient to move on the bank and return to Monterey. Rio is blamed for the ensuing robbery and Dad arrests him, threatening him with hanging. Pellicer visits Rio in jail and helps him escape and this leads to a fight between Rio and Dad, during which Dad is killed. Promising Pellicer that he will return, Rio rides off into the sunset.

That, more or less, is the story as it appears on screen but it is based on a version very much shorter than the one Brando shot. The crew remained on location for six months with Brando investing his new role of director with every bit as much detail as he customarily brought to his acting. He monitored everything from the smallest costume detail to the behaviour of the sea on the Californian coastline. When

Brando cast the unknown Pina Pellicer as Dad Longworth's adopted daughter (and the object of Rio's love) in One-Eyed Jacks. *The actress was not destined for a long career — a few years later, she would commit suicide.*

working with the extras he demanded that each one of them give a rounded performance and he was tirelessly patient with all the leading actors, from the experienced Malden to the newcomer Pellicer. But his patience was expensive. Frank Rosenberg, who produced the film, recalled: '(Brando) pondered each camera set-up while 120 members of the company sprawled on the ground like battle-weary troops...every line every actor read, as well as every button on every piece of wardrobe got Brando's concentrated attention until he was completely satisfied. It took six months to film *One-Eyed Jacks* instead of the sixty days we had planned...he exposed more than one million feet of film, thereby hanging up a new world's record.' The film's cost stretched from the budgeted $1.8 million to almost $6 million, and Brando's 'first cut' lasted six hours. When Brando finished editing, the film ran four hours and forty minutes, a length which Paramount found completely unacceptable. The studio took over the edit and brought the running time down to two hours and twenty minutes. Brando, who laboured so long on the film, called the final result 'a potboiler' which would not help its commercial release in 1961.

In Brando's original version, Pellicer's character is killed in the final shoot-out, but Paramount wanted a more up-beat ending. The studio persuaded Brando to change it with the result that the last scene was re-shot more than a year after principal photography had been completed. There are many things to admire in the film, Brando's careful use of land and seascapes among them, but it is not possible to judge him as a director when so much of the film's final shaping was taken out of his hands. What is clear is that Brando was now settling in to an image of himself, an image he was trying to create to supplant the tired 'Slob' label that had been earlier attached to him. He had been unable to play Diestl's Christ-like martyrdom in *The Young Lions*, but his original plan was echoed in the scene in which Dad Longworth horsewhips Rio. With his arms stretched out and tied to a hitching-post, Brando is finally given his moment of symbolic crucifixion – or at least ritual scourging.

By the time *One-Eyed Jacks* was released, Brando had completed his next film as an actor. This time he was returning to the work of the man who had provided his first important role – Tennessee Williams, but their partnership this time was to prove a disappointment for them both.

Williams had been so entranced by Brando's performance in *Streetcar* that he wanted to create a role with the actor specifically in mind. After several false starts, he decided to re-work an old play with a view to bringing Brando together with Anna Magnani, the Italian actress who had won an Oscar for her performance in the film version of another Williams play, *The Rose Tattoo*. This was Magnani's first American film, although she had established an international reputation with her

Rio (Brando) confronts his former bank-robbing partner Dad Longworth (Karl Malden), now a 'respectable' sheriff.

95

Rio (Brando) shows his contempt for the authority of his treacherous ex-partner, sheriff Dad Longworth (Malden) (right). He is then horse-whipped by the sheriff before collapsing into this familiar crucifixion pose (below right), a popular Brando leitmotif

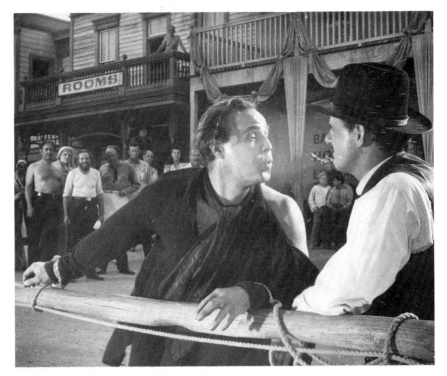

work in Roberto Rossellini's *Rome – Open City* which had heralded Italian neo-realism. Williams fashioned his 1940 play, *Battle of Angels* into *Orpheus Descending*, providing a strong role for Brando as the wandering musician, Val Xavier. Unfortunately, the role of Lady Torrance – which was written for Magnani – proved to be somewhat stronger and Brando declined the offer to appear in the play. If he feared that Magnani – a powerful and very physical actress – would dominate the play, he need not have worried. She also declined, claiming pressure of work in Italy but also nervous of playing a demanding stage role in English.

It was some time later that Martin Jurow, Magnani's American agent, approached Williams with a proposal to make a film version of the play. This time, said Jurow, Magnani would definitely agree to play Lady Torrance and overtures could be made to Brando who felt much more secure on film. With the difficulties of his divorce from Anna Kashfi – his settlement payments to her exceeded $500,000 and this was augmented by $1,000 a month for Christian – and the debacle of *One-Eyed Jacks* putting further financial pressure on him, Brando found it difficult to decline a second time. He still had his reservations, finding the role of Val to be underwritten and overshadowed by Williams' continued confusion of Brando with Stanley Kowalski, but he needed the money and the project had some promising aspects. Not the least of these was the hiring of Sidney Lumet as director. Lumet had established an impressive reputation as a director in live television and he had himself been an actor for many years, taking over Brando's role in Luther Adler's production of *A Flag is Born*.

Williams' play had been re-titled *The Fugitive Kind*, and the supporting cast included Joanne Woodward, Victor Jory and Maureen Stapleton. It was the second time Stapleton (who had played the lead in the stage version of *The Rose Tattoo*) had surrendered a leading role to Magnani. Woodward was cast as Carol Cutrere, the small town nymphomaniac who becomes Lady Torrance's rival.

Lumet spent two weeks rehearsing his cast at the Palladium Ballroom on Broadway and, from the very beginning, tensions began to surface. Magnani disliked the idea of rehearsing, fearing that it would staunch her spontaneity; Brando, on the other hand, relished the idea of preparing in such detail. Williams and his co-writer, Meade Roberts, seemed unable to help Lumet overcome the problems presented by the very different approaches of the lead actors. After a time, the difficulties began to affect the rest of the cast.

Maureen Stapleton set the scene for Donald Spoto, one of Williams' biographers: 'There we were, in this dance hall... The first week, Marlon and Anna and Joanne rehearsed alone. The second week, the rest of us were called in. Marlon sat there, mumbling his lines in a barely audible whisper. Anna refused to reply. Joanne was unsure what was going on. I had known Marlon since our days in the Drama Workshop at the New School in 1945, so I wasn't afraid to say something to him. Finally, after we read our first scene and I couldn't hear anything being said, I said, "I think I'm going deaf! You guys may be geniuses, but I have to hear what you're saying!" I was surprised Tenn didn't speak up and tell *them* to speak up. That night he and Frankie [Merlo, Williams' lover] came over to my house, and I said, "Tenn, you've got the muscle and the clout! Tell them what has to happen for this thing to work!" But he said, "Oh, I'm just an old faggot to them." '

The sentiments Williams expressed to Stapleton reflect his early disenchantment with *The Fugitive Kind* and also indicate his exasperation with the egocentricities of star actors. Certainly, the differences between Brando and Magnani were heightened by their individual egos, but Lumet has gone on record as identifying Magnani as the cause for most concern.

'I thought Marlon was brilliant in [*The Fugitive Kind*]. His scenes with Joanne Woodward contained some of the best acting he's ever done,' said the director in an interview with the *New York Times*. Of Magnani, he said that she had reached 'a very sad state in her life', adding 'that great talent had a great problem, and it was vanity. Suddenly, she was worried about the way she looked. The whole staging had to be shifted, and there were things Anna literally refused to do. But Marlon was Herculean – very giving – and yet he bore the brunt of the blame.'

The excesses of *One-Eyed Jacks* had clearly reaped their own bitter harvest, in that Brando would now be accounted responsible for any problem that might arise in one of his films. His working methods would increasingly be called into question or dismissed as eccentric and self-indulgent. It would be a long time before Brando would again work with a director who understood and respected him as Lumet did. 'He's extraordinarily knowledgeable about his own instrument,' Lumet said, 'and like all people who are, he therefore knows that his talent and ability have to be put into place. Marlon works in a fascinating way, by a process of elimination, constantly questioning why a point couldn't be made this way or that way. Primarily what he's doing is eliminating any other possibility of how to commit himself, it's thrilling to watch it. And it's thrilling to argue with him, and help him to channel that extraordinary motor into the place that the script demands.'

Brando was unhappy with the film from the start. He had agreed to do it only because he needed the money, and the fee of $1 million helped him to overcome his objections to the script. He had already explained his reservations to Tennessee Williams when *Orpheus Descending* was being constantly re-written, but he was never entirely convinced by the character of Val Xavier. Brando's engagement in the role had ousted the producer's original choice, Tony Franciosa. Franciosa had co-starred with Magnani in her second American film, *Wild is the Wind* (which failed at the box office) and he had become her lover. Magnani's insistence that Franciosa be cast as Val Xavier evaporated when she heard of Brando's interest. She could see the attraction of having Brando as her co-star but it soon became apparent that they could not find a balance for their different working methods. Once again, Brando found his slow approach at odds with a co-star who preferred to work quickly. But unlike Sinatra and Glenn Ford, Magnani decided to beat Brando at his own game. If Brando insisted on four takes, she would ask for a fifth. Such game-playing could only increase the tension on the set and made the Brando-Magnani love scenes especially difficult to film.

Nevertheless, the film has an integrity that is enhanced by the black and white photography of Boris Kaufman (who had shot *On the Waterfront*) and it remains one of the more successful film versions of Williams' work. If its box office performance was disappointing, this is no reflection on Brando's performance which is an intelligent distillation of aspects of his past screen personae which help flesh out the enigmatic Val Xavier. The very fact that he was drawing on his established 'image' may have led Brando to feel that he was going backward with the film, and the generally negative critical and public response probably added to that impression.

Brando was in urgent need of a change of pace, and things were certainly changing in Hollywood. New directors were coming to films from television (Lumet was one such) and many successful television plays had been remade for the big screen. But television was, in every other respect, the enemy camp. There was a demand at the big studios to make the kind of film that would outstrip the paltry offerings of the tube. At Metro-Goldwyn-Mayer, plans were laid to film a wide-screen, colour remake of one of the studio's greatest early successes, *Mutiny on the Bounty*. Filmed in 1936 with Clark Gable and Charles Laughton as the mutineer Fletcher Christian and the cruel Captain William Bligh, this was a story with proven audience appeal and one which would lend itself to being re-told for a new generation.

The success of their colour remake of *Ben Hur* (which won eleven Oscars in 1960) confirmed for MGM the notion that a subsequent remake of one of its properties could reap substantial benefits, and the search began for the best possible cast. Despite the failure of *The Fugitive Kind*, and the rumours that circulated about Brando's excesses as a director, MGM were so keen to have him as the star of *Mutiny on the Bounty* (playing whichever role he preferred) that they went so far as to offer him artistic control of the project. It was to be an expensive offer, both for the studio and, ultimately, for Brando.

Brando as Val Xavier with Anna Magnani in The Fugitive Kind, *Sidney Lumet's version of the Tennessee Williams play* Orpheus Descending.

7

The miscast mutineer

Brando as Fletcher Christian in Mutiny on the Bounty. *This costume shot (right) for Christian's post-mutiny appearance catches much of the posturing vanity which mars Brando's performance.*

THE IDEA of filming a new version of *Mutiny on the Bounty* came from the director, John Sturges, who also suggested Brando for one of the leading roles. MGM assigned the project to Aaron Rosenberg to compensate him after he was denied the opportunity to produce the studio's Cinerama epic, *How the West Was Won.* The script was to be written by the British novelist Eric Ambler, who had proved his grasp of maritime subjects with his screenplay for *The Cruel Sea.* Sol C. Siegel, MGM's chief executive, was convinced that Brando would be an excellent choice for the film, but he and Rosenberg felt that the subject matter called for a British director. Carol Reed was approached and, on the strength of the Ambler script, readily agreed. Once Brando had signed up to play Christian, Reed would contact his own favourite actor, Trevor Howard, to take on the role of Captain Bligh.

It must have looked marvellous on paper: Carol Reed directing the story of the Bounty from a script by Eric Ambler and with Brando and Howard in the leading roles. But problems began to arise very early on, and the film eventually cost MGM $27 million and brought the studio near to bankruptcy. In 1960, fighting a rearguard action against television, many film studios were inclined to invest their hopes in the box office appeal of one or two stars, believing that the name above the title would be sufficient to draw audiences. This sometimes led to the upsetting of the collaborative balance during the making of the film, and MGM must be accounted very foolish to turn over so much control on *Mutiny on the Bounty* to one actor, no matter how talented he was. As a result, much of the blame for the film's excesses has been laid at Brando's door, and there is no doubt that he must take some responsibility.

101

Even before he was approached by MGM, Brando had some connection with their earlier film version of the Bounty story. During the filming of *Viva Zapata!* he had become romantically involved with the actress who had played Fletcher Christian's Tahitian lover opposite Clark Gable. Her name was Maria Castenada, but she was better known by her professional name of Movita. She and Brando saw each other intermittently from 1955 until his marriage to Kashfi. After that marriage failed, Brando became involved with Movita again and married her in June 1960, just before shooting was to start on *Mutiny*. He was seven years younger than his new bride, who was pregnant with Brando's second son, Miko. Their romance did not long survive the wedding which seems to have been intended simply to legitimise the child. Eight years later, Brando had his marriage to Movita annulled – strange, in view of the fact that they had a child together but permissible under law because the marriage itself was not consummated.

Brando was not interested in a straight remake of *Mutiny on the Bounty*. From his point of view, the story became really interesting when the mutineers reached Pitcairn's Island and began to fight amongst themselves. The idea of a group of men attaining a virtual paradise and then destroying it yielded dramatic possibilities that had not been explored in the earlier film. Eric Ambler's script had given short shrift to this aspect of the story so Rosenberg called in other writers to flesh out a version which would have more appeal for Brando. By the time shooting started in October, 1960 the script had been revised by Borden Chase and William Driskill, and another writer Charles Lederer, had been brought into the project. Brando still wasn't satisfied but nevertheless location shooting began in Tahiti.

Beside Trevor Howard, the cast was filled with a number of first-rate British and Irish character actors: Richard Haydn, Hugh Griffith, Percy Herbert, Noel Purcell, Gordon Jackson and, given third billing after Brando and Howard, Richard Harris. *The Bounty* itself, or at least the painstakingly constructed replica of the famous ship, was late in arriving on the location, so Carol Reed was forced to shoot scenes in which it did not appear. Some members of the cast and crew were stricken with mild tropical illnesses and the problems were compounded when the weather took a turn for the worse. Reed worked well with Howard and encouraged him to give a detailed portrayal of Bligh which would not show him as the stereotypical tyrant. He was not happy, though, with Brando's determination to play Christian as a dandified fop. But Brando, not Reed, held the power on the set and his interpretation was not to be challenged.

Trevor Howard's biographer, Vivienne Knight, described the filming of the first scene between Howard and Brando: 'It was Trevor's scene, with five pages of dialogue for him and a few words for Brando. Every time Trevor hit his lines, Brando fluffed. They went on for eight takes,

Brando with his second wife Movita (Maria Castenada) posing for photo-booth shots.

Fletcher Christian (Brando) resists the temptation to strike Captain Bligh with the cat o'nine tails (left). Despite his romance with Tarita, Brando took his ex-wife Movita (below) to the Hollywood premiere of Mutiny. *Ironically, she had starred with Clark Gable in the 1935 version of the film.*

an unheard-of number for Trevor. Then, when Brando felt that Trevor might be off-key, he threw his line back. It was one of the oldest, and dirtiest, tricks in the actor's manual.'

Vivienne Knight's book is unashamedly partisan, but anybody who studies Brando's performance in *On the Waterfront* can witness this combative behaviour in his scenes with Rod Steiger. Howard was a solid, intelligent actor who was more than a match for any competitor. Against him, Brando looks all too often like an embodiment of Peter O'Toole's description of film acting as 'farting about in disguises'. From the very beginning, Brando's portrayal of Fletcher Christian was marked by a camp exaggeration that led to it becoming his most successful comic performance.

Reed found Brando's working method difficult but appeared prepared to compromise. According to Vivienne Knight, he waved aside complaints from the other actors with the words: 'There's nobody like Marlon.' For years, critics and colleagues had been telling Brando that he was special, different from the rest, and this was now becoming an excuse for his behaviour. Brando believed his own publicity – worse still, MGM and Carol Reed believed it. This would make it very easy for Brando to become a scapegoat for all the problems and the subsequent financial failure of *Mutiny on the Bounty*; but it was MGM who insisted on calling him a genius and allowing him to control their project. All he did was take them at their word. A genius, of course, sets his own

Hollwood veteran Lewis Milestone replaced Carol Reed as director of Mutiny on the Bounty *and received the screen credit, but it soon became clear that the overall power lay with Brando.*

standards. If Brando chose to change lines during the course of a scene, that was fine – he was a genius. Similarly, nobody at the studio seemed perturbed by his habit of having his lines written on cue cards which were often affixed to other actors' costumes. Howard was quoted as finding Brando 'unprofessional and ridiculous'. In ten years, he had gone from being a brilliant young talent to just another spoilt movie star.

When the conflict arose over interpretation of the story, Carol Reed found himself without any real authority. He was at odds with MGM's concept of the film, but MGM was consulting with Brando on every change. For Reed, this was a curious way to make a film but it was clear which way the studio would go if it had to choose between its star or its director. MGM paid Reed $200,000 and, much to the dismay of Trevor Howard and the British contingent, removed him from the film. In his place came Lewis Milestone, the Hollywood veteran whose most famous film was the anti-war classic *All Quiet On the Western Front*, made in 1931. Brando had great respect for the pacifist sympathies expressed in that film, and he welcomed Milestone's involvement in *Mutiny on the Bounty*. The respect did not, however, extend to any lessening of his artistic grip on the film and it quickly became apparent that he had no better rapport with Milestone than he had had with Reed.

Milestone himself was shocked to discover that so little of the film had been completed when he arrived. The unit had been at work for months but script problems, combined with the late arrival of the ship and the uncertain weather, had prevented any real progress. The question of directorial authority was again raised and quickly settled. Milestone, like everyone else, was expected to defer to Brando. According to the Irish actor Keith McConnell, who played James Morrison in the film, it was Trevor Howard who clarified the position for Milestone when the director tackled him for coming in slow on his lines in a long scene with Brando. 'Is there any kind of problem?' Milestone asked. 'Oh, no,' said Howard, 'there's no *problem*. I admire Mr. Brando's work very much, as do we all. And the dialogue he is creating as we go along is, I am sure, very good. The only *difficulty* is that I never know when he has finished.'

With Brando in such a controlling position, Milestone soon realised that the director's role was little more than that of a window-dresser. Rather than quit the film, he thought it best to wait until MGM fired him – as they would then have to pay him off. The studio did not wish to go to the trouble of finding yet another director so they kept Milestone on, even though he finally decided to abandon directing entirely, turning up on set to read magazines or doze off, leaving the shooting to others like Brando or the producer, Aaron Rosenberg. At one point, the cinematographer Robert L. Surtees was ready for a take when the operator was heard to shout: 'Would somebody please wake up the director – he's in the shot!'

Brando's interest in the South Seas location of Mutiny *was genuine and he spent much of his spare time photographing the Tahitian 'extras'.*

Given the absurd conditions of its making, it is remarkable that *Mutiny on the Bounty* is not totally unwatchable. In fact, it remains a very entertaining film – albeit one which is entirely dominated by Brando's idiosyncratic Fletcher Christian. His wicked caricature of an upper-class Englishman is wittily drawn, enjoyable to watch and immensely selfish. Not since *On the Waterfront* had Brando been so lovingly favoured by the camera, allowing him to dominate scenes which rightfully belonged to other actors. At one point, prior to the mutiny, Richard Harris and Hugh Griffith have a scene with Trevor Howard where two seamen are putting the crew's grievances to the captain. Brando overhears the beginnings of the conversation from his cabin. It could, and should be an effective scene which allows Christian to become further aware of Bligh's unreasonable attitude to the crew. He belongs on the edge of the scene, the burden of it lying with Harris, Griffith and Howard. Unfortunately, Christian is seen in his cabin wearing a preposterously large silk dressing-gown topped by a matching night-cap, and he is smoking an enormous clay pipe. He looks like a pantomime character and it is impossible to look at anyone else when he is on screen. When he leaves the shot, the audience is still reacting to his costume with disbelief and laughter and so its attention continues to be drawn away from the main characters, their dialogue and the real drama of the scene.

There is something else about *Mutiny on the Bounty* which recalls *On the Waterfront* and, to some extent, *The Young Lions*. In each of these films, Brando plays a man who tries not to become involved in a situation which disturbs him. When he does become involved, his actions somehow redeem him. Terry Malloy, Christian Diestl and Fletcher Christian all begin as self-centred charmers who are confronted by others and stirred into action. Terry is confronted by Edie, Christian Diestl is confronted by his French girlfriend, Françoise, and Fletcher Christian is stung by the disdain of his old friend and junior officer, Ned Young (excellently played by Tim Seely). Each of these confrontations marks a turning point for the character whose watchfulness increases thereafter.

Given that Brando had some say in the script development of *The Young Lions* and *Mutiny on the Bounty*, it is quite possible that he was deliberately pushing his characters into schematic repetitions of Terry Malloy's redemption. But Diestl and Fletcher Christian are both intelligent men and their changes of heart are less convincing because they are heightened and falsified. Nevertheless, both roles give Brando the opportunity to react, something he can do with exceptional subtlety. What goes wrong with his Fletcher Christian is that he jumps between two separate characterisations and never quite convinces that the humane and authoritative Lieutenant occupies the same body as the facetious dandy.

That said, there is much to relish in Brando's performance – not least of which are the outrageous quips which pepper his dialogue. When a particularly nasty seaman has informed on one of his shipmates, Christian asks him: 'Was there anything else you wished to discuss – early Renaissance sketching perhaps?' After the mutiny he confides to another seaman that he has 'a slight wish to be dead, which I'm sure will pass'. If these seem inappropriate on the page it is never clear in performance whether Brando is sending the whole thing up or genuinely aiming at fleshing out his character. What is strange is to find Brando being so impeccably funny in a dramatic role when he is frequently inept in comedy.

Brando's plan to have the film concentrate on the aftermath of the mutiny went unrealised. Instead, the mutineers were shown settling in to their island paradise only to be urged by Christian to return to England and state their case in court. The thought that Christian might somehow force them to return home against their will leads Mills (Richard Harris) to set fire to the *Bounty*. Christian rushes aboard to save the ship's sextant, but is severely burned and carried ashore by his friends. Dying, Christian assures Mills that he had no intention of acting against the men's wishes, and he swears love to the young Tahitian girl (Tarita) who has become his lover on the island. The film ends with Christian dead and the wrecked *Bounty* ablaze and sinking

Brando looking elegant here as Fletcher Christian, although for most of the film his outlandishly foppish garb made his Christian hard to take seriously.

in the background.

This ending was one of a dozen that had been written, discussed and – in some cases – filmed. Lewis Milestone was the credited director on the film but there seems to have been no one hand on the helm. Brando, Rosenberg and Surtees took turns to direct scenes and Ben Hecht and Billy Wilder were both involved in late work on the script. The location shooting dragged on, grinding to a halt on several occasions while lengthy script conferences were called and screenings were held of the available footage. At a Presidential dinner in California, John F. Kennedy turned to Billy Wilder – whose involvement in *Bounty* was not publicly known – and asked 'When are they going to finish *Mutiny on the Bounty*?' According to Milestone, Charles Lederer would write up the script on a daily basis and arrived with new pages which were then discussed with Brando and Rosenberg. Eventually, Brando and Rosenberg fell out and Milestone – unable to bear it any longer – gave up completely and left the picture. The

A hero's death: Fletcher Christian braves the flames of the burning Bounty *to salvage the ship's sextant.*

idea of Christian's heroic death came from Billy Wilder – it pleased Brando who had seen a rough cut of the film in July, 1962, and liked everything but the ending Milestone had shot. Wilder insisted that he should not be credited and the same proviso was imposed by George Seaton who actually shot this last section when it was obvious that Milestone would not return to the location.

When Twentieth-Century Fox blamed Elizabeth Taylor for their losses on *Cleopatra*, MGM eagerly followed suit by blaming Brando for wrecking *Mutiny on the Bounty*. Their complaints gained extra currency as a result of an article by Bill Davidson in the *Saturday Evening Post*. Entitled 'The Mutiny of Marlon Brando', the article gave full vent to the resentment that had built up against Brando among members of the unit. It portrayed him as a crazy egoist who was intent on bankrupting the studio and alienating his colleagues. It provided MGM with the justification they needed and dealt a massive blow to Brando's standing in the film industry. Suddenly, he was worse than a brilliant eccentric – he was dangerously expensive.

Brando had been contracted to *Mutiny on the Bounty* before the release of *The Fugitive Kind* and *One-Eyed Jacks* but now the on-screen experiences of his last three films had accumulated to give him a reputation he could not afford. There was a possibility that MGM would sue him, just as Fox had sued Taylor for on-set misconduct; but they did not really have a case and Milestone – who would have been their strongest witness – refused to testify against Brando. When Brando sued the publishers of the *Saturday Evening Post* in January 1963, he received support from an unexpected quarter – Trevor Howard.

The film was not able to match the drama of the 1935 version and the popular image of Captain Bligh would remain that presented by Charles Laughton. Trevor Howard's skilful portrayal of a driven martinet was wasted against Brando's buffoonery, and the film was a flop. The troubled history of the film's making is reflected in the finished product. Brando, whatever his excesses, is clearly marching to a different drummer as Christian and the film breaks unevenly into two sections – with a colourful entr'acte in Tahiti. On the voyage out, Fletcher Christian is a comic character whose authority is questionable – in the section leading up to the mutiny, he has changed into a watchful man, wrestling with his conscience and awaiting – even delaying – the moment of action. This is what Brando does best and it is what made his portrayals of Terry Malloy and Christian Diestl so compelling. But the power of the love scenes between Brando and Eva Marie Saint in *On the Waterfront* was not apparent in either *The Young Lions* or *Mutiny on the Bounty*. When Fletcher Christian sets off to woo Maimiti (Tarita), the chief's daughter, it is to the strains of 'Rule Britannia', and their dialogue ('No, no, Fletcher,' she

Fletcher Christian (Brando) woos Princess Maimiti (Tarita Teriipaia). Tarita, a 19-year-old local Tahitian beauty became Brando's real-life lover and third wife.

protests; 'Yes, yes, Fletcher,' he insists) is frankly ludicrous. In reality, Brando and Tarita would become lovers – and this relationship would doubtless remain his only happy souvenir of the filming.

The repercussions of the *Post* article were to have a serious effect on Brando's career, robbing him of the power to control his projects. Even after MGM made conciliatory statements in the press and Brando appeared on the publicity trail for *Bounty*, the received opinion was that the actor was simply far more trouble than he was worth.

Ironically, Brando had elected to do *Mutiny on the Bounty* as against another epic story which he feared would have tied him up too long on location, *Lawrence of Arabia*. David Lean's film made a star of Peter O'Toole as T. E. Lawrence, but Brando and Albert Finney had originally been announced for the lead in the film which was produced by Sam Spiegel. In the wake of the *Bounty* fiasco, Spiegel remarked that Brando 'would have been impossible for Lawrence'. He summed up the prevailing Hollywood attitude to Brando: 'When I made *On the Waterfront* with Marlon he was magnificent. Now he has become a tortured person and in turn a tortured actor.' Spiegel was not the only one of Brando's past associates to decide that the actor was a spent force but, happily, others were prepared to ease him back on the path to acceptance.

Chief among them was Jay Kanter at MCA. The agency had moved into television production but was required, in accordance with government legislation, to abandon its client list. It did so, and followed this action with the acquisition of Universal Pictures and a move into full-scale film and television production. In 1962, with *Mutiny on the Bounty* still incomplete, Universal Pictures signed Brando to a long-term contract, beginning with the leading role in *The Ugly American*.

Brando himself had bought the rights to William J. Lederer and Eugene Burdick's novel for Pennebaker Productions with a view to developing it with his partner, George Englund. The book raised questions about American foreign policy which Brando found pertinent and in urgent need of achieving wider circulation through the cinema. Set in the fictitious country of Sarkhan, it was a stern critique of America's growing involvement in Vietnam. The line taken by the book and the film, that American self-interest resulted in a blinkered approach to overseas relations, would lead Brando into further controversy. By associating himself with such a film he was perceived as anti-American.

In fact, Brando had already shown himself to be un-American (not in the paranoid sense applied by HUAC, but inasmuch as he was far from the typical American abroad). While the British contingent on *Bounty* may have found Brando a difficult colleague, it must be said that they had their own – far from attractive – reputations to contend with. Howard, Griffith and Harris were not known at that time for their temperance (indeed, Griffith succeeded in getting himself thrown out of Tahiti for his drunken behaviour) and they did not share Brando's enthusiasm for the South Pacific. His interest was undoubtedly heightened by his relationship with Tarita Teriipaia. A nineteen-year old of Chinese-Tahitian origin, Tarita, was one of several local girls who were tested for the role of Maimiti. She had never acted before – nor would she again – but she was a fine natural dancer and needed only to have her teeth fixed to conform to Hollywood's ideal of South Seas beauty. She was clearly Brando's ideal too, for only a year after filming ended he and Tarita had the first of their two children, a son called Tehitou. At about that time, Brando purchased Tetiaroa, a group of thirteen islands to the north of Tahiti. In 1969, Tarita gave birth to Brando's daughter Cheyenne. Over the years Tetiaroa would become a refuge for Brando and the members of his extended family – but never more poignantly than it became for Cheyenne in 1990.

Throughout Brando's career, he has shown a lively interest in the cultures and the peoples he has encountered on various locations. When this has been remarked upon, it is usually cited as evidence of his need for distraction. But it is consistent with his continued work with UNICEF and UNESCO. It was in the sixties, when the initial impact of his screen talent had been absorbed and his acting career seemed to be in decline, that Brando's political interests became apparent. He began more openly to associate himself with causes – civil

Brando's political convictions were by now becoming more apparent. Here he is in London in 1964, attending a debate on apartheid and talking with Mr. Abdul, a South African Indian and prominent anti-apartheid activist.

rights and the condition of the American Indians were paramount –
and to seek out projects which in some way reflected these interests.
At the same time, he became aware of the limitations of acting as a
means of expression and he was drawn more often to writing (an area
of activity in which he has yet to distinguish himself).

It was his social consience, as much as his need to regain favour in
Hollywood, that led Brando to *The Ugly American* and the film would
mark a further turning-point in his career. With it, he would turn his
back on the iconographic roles of earlier years: it was his farewell to
youth. Not before time, it might be said, for Brando was nearing
forty and had reached a point in his career when he should no longer
be concerned with proving his versatility. The only thing he had to
prove now was his ability to work with others in a productive way that
was not time-consumingly expensive. Thanks to the bad publicity that
surrounded the shooting of *Mutiny on the Bounty* the choices open to
him had been reduced.

Nevertheless, Brando continued to initiate idealistic projects and his
belief that he could carry them through can only have been the result
of an uneasy mixture of naivety and egotism. Egotism is a common
enough quality among actors, and it is found in writers and directors
too – and it is often mistakenly perceived as strength – a fact which
may account for the infrequency of Brando's work with really first-class
talents. Among Brando's most documented fears is that of 'being
manipulated' and the manipulative element of *On the Waterfront*
can hardly have escaped him. Kazan was far from the only Hollywood
director to use manipulation of both actor and audience as part of his

After finishing Mutiny,
*Brando was so enamoured
with the South Seas
location that he purchased
Tetiaroa, a group of
thirteen islands to the
north of Tahiti. Here,
Brando relaxes on his
island retreat.*

111

technique and his direction of Brando as Malloy had had a long-term effect on the actor (as can be seen from those crypto-Malloys, Christian Diestl and Fletcher Christian). Brando had been at his best when he trusted his director; after *Bounty* he trusted very few people, and those he did trust were people he could dominate. His belief that good work could be done under these conditions demonstrates his naivety.

In *The Ugly American* Brando plays Harrison Carter MacWhite, a journalist who is appointed American Ambassador to Sarkhan. MacWhite knew the country during the Second World War and, more significantly, he had become friends with Deong who is now a revolutionary nationalist. MacWhite's mission is to steer Sarkhan toward a course in keeping with American overseas interests and he finds Deong vigorously opposed to American plans for a 'Freedom Road' running into the north of the country. Sarkhan's premier, Kwen Sai, convinces MacWhite that Deong has fallen under the influence of the Communists who control the northern part of the country. In reality, Deong is politically unaligned and is simply intent on fighting imperialism – whether from America or the Communist bloc. It takes a long time for MacWhite to understand the true needs and desires of the people of Sarkhan and this leads him to find American attitudes uneducated and self-serving. After leading a successful revolt against Kwen Sai's government, Deong is assassinated by the Communists and MacWhite realises that his mission has been a misguided failure. He resigns his post and returns to the United States to give a bitter

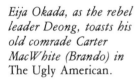

Eija Okada, as the rebel leader Deong, toasts his old comrade Carter MacWhite (Brando) in The Ugly American.

press conference in which he condemns American ignorance and complacency. The film ends with a shot of a man switching off his television and cutting short MacWhite's speech.

In 1963, American film audiences tended to reflect the attitude expressed in the last shot of the film and *The Ugly American* met with a lukewarm reception. It was certainly a courageous enterprise but it needed a directorial talent to match Brando's – something that George Englund did not have. As a result, the parallels with Vietnam are lost in the slow exposition and the establishment of a totally fictional landscape. The political climate was also unhelpful. America was enjoying the optimism of the Kennedy administration and, in the months ahead the country would be plunged into a period of extended mourning by the assassination of its youngest-ever President. By then, the views expressed in *The Ugly American* would be too bleak to contemplate.

As with *Sayonara*, Brando found himself paired with a celebrated Japanese actor. This time it was Eiji Okada who had gained international recognition for his performance in *Hiroshima, Mon Amour*. Okada was cast as Deong but his command of English was so limited that he was inevitably placed at an enormous disadvantage. The casting of an influential Thai journalist, Kukrit Pramoj, as the prime minister Kwen Sai was initiated by Brando and Englund who had been impressed with Pramoj's personality. In a way, this served to undermine Brando's avowed intention of presenting a realistic portrait of South-East Asia. By casting a Japanese and a Thai as members of the same nation, *The Ugly American* gave currency to the notion that all Easterners are basically the same.

Brando's performance as MacWhite – a decent man imprisoned by events – is unfortunately very dull. As so often in his portrayal of 'educated' characters, Brando adopts a curiously pursed-mouth way of speaking. There is nothing wrong with his diction – as Fred Zinnemann once remarked, Brando does not mumble, he is merely soft-spoken – but his voice has a tendency to start in the back of his throat and rarely gets beyond his teeth. His way of reflecting before a line – a raising of both eyebrows which causes an upward furrow on his brow – is frequently accompanied by a vague stare into the middle distance which makes him appear permanently distracted. Brando has had a tendency to run to fat since childhood and in *The Ugly American* he looks pudgy, his face almost characterless. Despite the presence of a fussy little moustache, Brando's face here has all the expression of a soft-boiled egg.

What the film did achieve was the establishment of Brando as a mature man, an authority figure, albeit flawed. It was a Brando that his public had not previously seen, that it did not really want to see, but it signalled a hopeful move away from his youthful excesses.

Brando strives for an air of authority as Harrison Carter MacWhite, American Ambassador to the fictional country Sarkhan in The Ugly American.

8

A star in eclipse

THERE is something slow, almost hesitant, in Brando's portrayal of Carter MacWhite. He looks like a man who is trying on a suit for the first time (which, cinematically speaking, Brando was) and who is unsure of the fit. Few actors have been seen thinking on screen as often as Brando, and this in part accounts for the apparent slowness of his performances. He gets the thought before the line or, sometimes, in the middle of it. Now this is something that many actors are told to do by their directors, it stops them from gabbling or coming in automatically on cue and it adds verisimilitude. At least, it should. But such a technique cannot work if the part has not been written in such a way that allows for it, and this is where Brando can sometimes destroy the dramatic intention of an author. It might be expected that Brando's naturalism would show up the artificialities of a script, but the opposite is often the case and Brando himself looks artificial and mannered. When called upon to act, he abandons all pretence of naturalism and becomes an outrageous ham.

For a long time there appeared to be no middle way for Brando. In both cases he had fallen into the actor's trap of relying on a tried and tested bag of tricks – looks, gestures, actions – that could be adapted to each performance. He did not attempt to learn his lines, becoming adept at reading cue-cards instead. The task of committing a difficult role to memory is arduous and boring for most actors, and many talented screen performers have tried to side-step the process by employing cue-cards (or 'idiot boards' as they are popularly known). Unfortunately Brando was a movie star who had been acclaimed as the best of his generation – even, absurdly, the best actor in cinema history, and few people were inclined to take him to task over the waning of his powers.

A Cecil Beaton portrait of the mature Brando. The open expression which characterised his previous sitting for Beaton has been replaced by one of guarded reserve.

114

The Ugly American was followed in 1964 by a film which contains one of Brando's worst performances, *Bedtime Story*. This charmless tale of a pair of con-men preying off women on the French Riviera allowed David Niven, an excellent farceur, to run rings around the totally miscast Brando. The film had originally been written by Stanley Shapiro as a vehicle for Cary Grant and Tony Curtis, who had proved an engaging duo in an earlier Shapiro script, *Operation Petticoat*. Shapiro had a successful record of frothy comedies for Universal with such titles as *Lover Come Back*, *Pillow Talk* and *That Touch of Mink*. But these required actors like Grant, Curtis, Tony Randall and Doris Day who were accomplished light comedians, or else amiable lightweights like Rock Hudson who were not at odds with the material. In a film like *Bedtime Story*, Brando is simply ungainly. After *Waterfront* his performances lacked precision, and that is the essence of comedy acting.

Brando and David Niven in action as conmen in the comedy Bedtime Story. *Brando described it as 'the only time I ever really enjoyed myself...God, Niven made me laugh so hard'.*

In reviewing *Bedtime Story*, Dwight MacDonald underlined Brando's inadequacy: 'He is an American soldier abroad who is a liar, swindler, blackmailer and – his specialty – a ruthless seducer (and impregnator) of women, his technique being to play on their sympathies as a lonely soldier boy far from home. A better actor might have made this heel amusing – seducers and con men have their comic aspects – but Brando makes us detest him as a slob and a bully; the pious smirk he puts on when he goes into the soldier-boy act is unappetising, as well as being amateurishy "indicative" acting.'

But making the film was a pleasure for Brando who told Lawrence Grobel in a 1979 *Playboy* interview that it was 'the only time I ever *really* enjoyed myself...God, [Niven] made me laugh so hard. We got the giggles like two girls at a boarding school. He finally had to ask me to go to my trailer, I couldn't stop laughing. We both thought it was such a funny script, a funny story.' In answer to Grobel's question 'would you have liked to do more comedy?' Brando answered flatly: 'No, I can't do comedy.'

The film did not match the success of Shapiro's earlier efforts, with Judith Crist in the *New York Herald Tribune* dismissing it as 'a vulgar soporific for the little-brained ones'. When it was remade in 1989 as *Dirty Rotten Scoundrels* with Michael Caine and Steve Martin it only won the support of Martin's fans. Brando's own fans (among whom Dwight MacDonald clearly did not number himself) were becoming accustomed to the disappointment that attended each new performance. Pauline Kael spoke for many when she wrote: 'Brando, our most powerful young screen actor, the only one who suggested tragic force, the major protagonist of contemporary American themes in the fifties, is already a self-parodying comedian.'

Brando in Bedtime Story.
Years later he told Playboy
magazine that he couldn't
act comedy.

There is no doubt that, by the mid-sixties, Brando's career was in crisis and it was difficult to imagine that he could ever climb out of the trough he had been encouraged to dig for himself. It was not entirely his fault; his talent had been oversold – when he needed guidance he was given only flattery and he compounded this by surrounding himself with mediocre talents. He could not be 'the major protagonist of contemporary American themes' if he was not prepared to work efficiently with comparable talents – writers, actors and directors who would demand something of him. His determination to prove his versatility served only to expose his limitations.

There are a great many American actors who were more versatile than Brando: James Cagney (one of the greatest exponents of screen versatility); Melvyn Douglas; Jack Lemmon; Fredric March; Spencer Tracy – all actors able to switch from comedy to drama with ease. But the shadows cast by Kowalski and Malloy were long and indelible. When the conditions were right, Brando was matchless: it was impossible to imagine someone else playing his role and he was a great dramatic actor. The promise contained in those early performances had yet to be fulfilled and audiences were becoming tired of waiting. It was as if the performances themselves were not enough. Lesser actors were allowed to grow as their careers progressed and they were forgiven the occasional lack-lustre performance – in short, their careers were better managed. Paul Newman, for example, began by sharing Brando's ineptitude for comedy but was better able to learn so that his roles in *Butch Cassidy and the Sundance Kid* and *The Sting* showed a lightness of touch. But Newman's best roles were tailored for his limitations while Brando's limitations were rarely admitted – the prevailing attitude in Hollywood remained one of 'this man can do anything'.

There was another threat to Brando's bankability at the time of *Bedtime Story*. He had become openly allied to political causes that were not universally popular in the United States. His avowed support for Civil Rights activists like Martin Luther King led to an unofficial boycott of his films in the southern states. Other actors with liberal views, such as Paul Newman and Gregory Peck, could withstand similar boycotts because their films performed well at the box office, but Brando films were booking badly throughout the country and his position became progressively weaker.

Brando's next film was little more than an exercise in damage limitation, but it contained the seeds of something much greater. In 1964, with his case against the *Saturday Evening Post* still unresolved, Brando was approached by Aaron Rosenberg to star opposite Yul Brynner in *Morituri*, a wartime thriller under the direction of the German Bernhard Wicki. Wicki had been brought to Hollywood on the strength of his international success with his film, *The Bridge*, and his European view would have held some appeal for Brando. What held even more appeal was that Rosenberg, the producer of *Mutiny on the Bounty*, was prepared to work again with the alleged destroyer of the MGM epic. Such a proposition strengthened Brando's case against the *Post*. With Brando's encouragement, Trevor Howard was invited to play an important 'guest' role in the film and he brought with him two friends who had also played in *Bounty*. The idea of Marlon Brando working again with the producer and three of the actors from *Mutiny on the Bounty* made nonsense of the *Post*'s story and the case was settled out of court, and in Brando's favour.

A secondary reason for Brando to accept *Morituri* was also financial. Explaining his position to one reporter, he said; 'It is like a car and the oil dipstick. You look at it once in a while, and find you need oil. Well, every so often I look at my financial condition and I find I need money, so I do a good-paying picture. You see, I have three households to support and I pay alimony to two women.' Brando was operating well and truly from within the Hollywood system. As far as his film career was concerned, he had become a thorough-going cynic. Tired of discussions about acting – which he dismissed as trivial – he reserved his few serious comments for those subjects he believed to be of greater importance: Civil Rights, Third World poverty and the plight of the American Indians.

With all this in mind, the attraction of working with an admired European director came low on Brando's list of priorities. In any case, the script of *Morituri* was by Daniel Taradash who had also written the less than distinguished dialogue for *Desirée*. In more senses than one, *Morituri* was old ground for Brando.

Once again, he was cast as a 'good German'. Robert Crain is an anti-Nazi pacifist who is forced out of exile and pressed into working

Trevor Howard was briefly reunited with Brando for Morituri.

as a saboteur and double-agent for the British. In order to prepare a German merchant ship for capture, Crain is required to pose as an SS officer sailing on board the ship as an observer. He quickly comes to respect the ship's captain Mueller (Yul Brynner) while having to feign an alliance with the openly Nazi first officer. En route from Japan to France with a cargo of rubber, the ship takes on board a number of captured American sailors and a Jewish girl (Janet Margolin) to whom Crain reveals his true position. Together they try to facilitate a mutiny but Crain's identity is exposed over the radio and the Nazi sympathisers on board take command with the first officer at their head. Crain appeals to Mueller to resume command, but Mueller's patriotism overwhelms his distaste for Nazism. As Crain faces up to the limitations of his pacifism, Mueller finally begins to question himself.

Morituri has all the makings of a first-class thriller. It is atmospherically shot in black and white by Conrad Hall, mostly on location at sea and the performances of Brando, Brynner and Howard (seen only briefly as the Intelligence Officer who recruits Crain) are thoughtful. Bernhard Wicki was in sympathy with the story, which was based on a novel by Werner Joerg Luedecke (himself a former German naval attaché whose partial Jewishness resulted in his being shipped from Tokyo to Germany and thence to a punishment battalion on the Russian front). The main trouble lies with the ponderous dialogue and the awful pretentiousness that hangs around so many Hollywood attempts to convey an 'important

Robert Crain (Brando) is forced to reveal his true identity to Esther (Janet Margolin) in Morituri.

119

message'. What might have been a powerful film if made in Wicki's native Germany became self-consciously worthy and undramatic. This was, after all, a product of Twentieth-Century Fox and it had to appeal to the American audience. In that respect, the title itself presented a problem. '*Morituri te salutant*', says Brando as he sets off on his mission – 'those about to die salute you'. It may not necessarily require a classical education to recognise these words as the famous cry of the gladiators in the Circus Maximus of Ancient Rome, but *Morituri* sounded obscure, not to mention vaguely Japanese, to most of the American public. An attempt to clarify matters by changing the title to *The Saboteur; Codename Morituri* did little to help the film at the box office.

For all the intelligence of his performance as Crain, Brando was now happily playing the familiar movie star game of Getting Away with Murder. He engaged Taradash in a series of script conferences that led to Brando rewriting whole scenes. 'His idea of rewriting was "How would Marlon Brando act in the situation?" ' complained Taradash. 'It was like having a script conference with a foetus.' Taradash may not have been the best screenwriter in Hollywood, but he was a professional and had won an Oscar for his work on *From Here to Eternity*.

Brando even brought other actors in on the re-writing, according to Aaron Rosenberg. Brando's old friend Wally Cox had joined the cast as the ship's drug-addicted doctor, together with Brando's *Arms and the Man* co-star William Redfield, and Rosenberg accused Brando of taking his friends into his trailer to continue the script revisions. This resulted in the constant up-staging of other actors. In one of Janet Margolin's most important scenes, Brando crosses aimlessly to gaze out of a porthole when the scene as written had him sitting quietly on his bunk. When Taradash asked Rosenberg to explain Brando's move, Rosenberg retorted: 'Because his goddamned lines were on the idiot board outside the porthole!'

One impartial observer on the set of *Morituri* was the film critic of the London *Evening Standard*, Alexander Walker. In his entertaining memoir, *It's Only a Movie, Ingrid*, Walker describes the shooting of a key scene between Brando and Trevor Howard. It was the scene in which Howard, as Colonel Statter of British Intelligence, is trying to persuade Robert Crain to leave his base in India and help the Allied war effort. 'As written,' Walker explains, 'the scene had been largely Howard's. He had virtually all the dialogue, hence ought to command most of the situation. Brando would have to retrieve what he could of it on reaction shots.'

Things might have turned out that way if Brando had not decided to 'improve' the scene with three inessential additions: a dog for him to play with, a young Asian girl to serve him tea, and an old phonograph for him to play music – all during Trevor Howard's speech. Brando was more powerful than Bernhard Wicki, so there was no question of these additions being over-ruled, and to some extent his demands seemed reasonable. Walker concedes that they gave the scene 'a tension it simply wouldn't have possessed had it been played straight in an even-handed way.' But it was just as easy to interpret the changes as being part of a power play, as Walker's description of the second take of the scene illustrates:

' "Action!" And again Brando fed the dog – while Howard was talking – ordered his tea – while Howard was talking – and commanded music – while Howard was talking. Only this time it didn't go quite as planned.

' "Vould you like to hear some music?" Brando walked across to the phonograph and made great play of selecting a record. But in placing it on the turntable, he fumbled it – and the disc fell on the floor...As the thick brittle disc hit the stone-flagged floor, it fragmented into a dozen pieces. "Shit!" said Brando. "Cut!" cried Wicki. Trevor Howard swivelled round, shot a glance of unholy glee at where he knew I was standing in the penumbra round the highly-lit set and cried, or rather crowed, "Just like *Mutiny on the Bounty*, my old love...Just like *Mutiny on the Bounty*." '

I do not believe, any more than Alexander Walker does, that Brando's elaborations of a scene are mere shows of egocentricity. Rather, he seems unable to accept the boundaries beyond which it is useless for any actor to tread. He pads around inside an inferior film like a caged lion, repeatedly tearing at the air or demolishing his surroundings in an effort to assert himself. But, finally, he is as firmly imprisoned as the lion – an ageing lion in a third-rate circus. The handlers and the circus owners are in overall control – he can maim them or kill them, but only at the cost of destroying himself. He cannot walk away or return to the wild. Of course, Garbo walked away – but she was a gazelle, not a lion, and her temperament differed from Brando's. Her beauty was her strongest point, and when that faded the public would simply have passed her by. Brando was different; no matter how old or ragged he might become, there was always the possibility that the lion would roar again.

As far as the public was concerned, throughout the sixties Brando was no more interesting than an animal act – and just as unfashionable. There were new movie heroes now – this was the age of James Bond (a role for which Brando was briefly considered). It was an age of affluence and optimism, of the kind of progress signalled by the conquest of space. It hardly mattered that this was also an especially violent decade for America, with Vietnam and the assassinations of the Kennedys, Martin Luther King, Malcolm X and Lincoln Rockwell – that was all the more reason for escapism. Brando was associated with a cathartic view of American life, but the public wanted something else, it wanted

121

happy endings. Anyway, Brando was only repeating himself.

In reality, it was the film producers – the circus owners – who were making Brando repeat himself by forcing him through the same old hoops. Just how far the actor had come from his rebellious beginnings would be demonstrated in his next role. As Sheriff Calder in *The Chase*, Brando was playing a similar character to that played by Robert Keith in *The Wild One* twelve years before: a decent, but fatally compromised, figure of authority.

Brando's star was on the wane when he appeared in The Chase *with the up-and-coming Robert Redford. Here, as Sheriff Calder, Brando takes Redford's Bubber Reeves into custody (below). A beaten Brando with Angie Dickinson (bottom).*

It was Sam Spiegel who cast Brando in the film. Spiegel had originally wanted Peter O'Toole to play Calder, but O'Toole was smart enough to realise that he was not ideally cast as a Texan and so Spiegel approached Brando. Brando now found himself stepping into O'Toole's shoes in a Spiegel film, just as O'Toole had once stepped into Brando's to play T. E. Lawrence. In both cases, O'Toole got the better part of the deal.

The Chase had begun life as a play by Horten Foote (author of *The Trip to Bountiful* and screenwriter of *To Kill a Mockingbird*). Directed by Jose Ferrer, the play had starred John Hodiak as Sheriff Calder and had been performed in New York in 1952. For the film version, Lillian Hellman was hired to write the screenplay, and Arthur Penn – whose film credits included *The Left-Handed Gun* and *The Miracle Worker* – was brought in to direct.

The story centres on a troubled Saturday night in the Texas town of Tarl, where the population are bracing themselves for the return of Bubber Reeves (Robert Redford) – newly escaped from the State Penitentiary where he has been incarcerated on a probably false charge. Bubber's wife, Anna (Jane Fonda) is having an affair with Jake Rogers (James Fox), once Bubber's best friend and son of Val Rogers (E. G. Marshall), the tycoon who controls the town and its sheriff. Sheriff Calder is one of those who believes Bubber to be innocent but he is conscious of having compromised his own integrity by protecting Val Rogers' corrupt business interests. To complicate matters, two of Rogers' employees (Richard Bradford and Robert Duvall) are planning a takeover and hope to strengthen their chances by getting to Bubber first and breaking the news of Anna's affair to him. All that Calder wants to do is keep everyone calm and bring Bubber in for a fair trial.

In Arthur Penn, Brando found the kind of strong, intelligent direction he needed and which helped him to give a tightly disciplined performance as Calder. He more than holds his own in demanding company for, aside from the ever-reliable Marshall, he was having to match his talent against some of the most highly regarded actors of a younger generation – Redford, Fonda and Duvall. But this time it is the film – and not Brando – which is excessive. It would be more than a little fanciful to claim that *The Chase* provides an unconscious comment on the state of Brando's career, but there is

'A decent but fatally compromised figure of authority' — *Brando as Sheriff Calder in* The Chase.

something allegorical in the sight of a man moving slowly through the mayhem and attempting to preserve his integrity while everyone around is bartering for his support. At one point, Calder sighs: 'What did I do to make all these people think they could buy me?' For a moment, it might not be the sheriff of Tarl speaking but Brando himself, reflecting on the venal tawdriness of Hollywood.

Lillian Hellman attempted to remove her name from the finished film, claiming that Penn and Spiegel re-worked her screenplay with two other writers of their choice (although Hellman received sole credit). 'Decision by democratic majority vote is a fine form of government,' Hellman observed, 'but it's a stinking way to create...What was intended as a modest picture about some aimless people on an aimless Saturday night got hot and large.' If the phrase 'aimless people on an aimless Saturday night' has a familiar feel to it, it is not surprising. *The Chase* is *The Wild One* grown older and fatter.

Actors do not have the privilege accorded to screenwriters – if they are dissatisfied with the way their work has been presented there is little point in having their names removed from the credits, they cannot remove their faces. The film actor, in particular, is at the mercy of the director and of the editor. It is not always possible to turn a bad performance into a good one in the cutting room, but it is an easy task to turn a good one into a mockery of itself. With

Bounty hunter Matt (Brando) defends himself in The Appaloosa *(known as* Southwest to Sonora *in Britain).*

this in mind, Brando's desire to control his performances becomes partially understandable. No director since Kazan had been interested in allowing his camera to be led by Brando's performance, so Brando had to force them to follow him. He did it in *Mutiny on the Bounty* and in *Morituri*. He did it, but subtly in *The Chase*, and trusted his director to follow. He was to be disappointed.

In fairness to Penn – who would soon achieve a resounding success with *Bonnie and Clyde* – he knew that the film had done a disservice to Brando. He encouraged Brando to improvise in an effort to liven up a script which he considered 'stilted and excessively expository'. These improvisations corresponded to scenes in the finished film but were never used – 'a great loss,' said Penn, 'of some of the best acting I'd ever witnessed.' In discussing the film's presentation of Sheriff Calder, Penn has observed: 'He was a man whose whole action in the picture was to hold on to a mature view and avoid an infantile, retaliatory aggressive stance. He had to try and cool it as best he could in a community which was somewhat infantile in its views. The sadness of the story is that Calder failed. The other sadness is that we failed Calder. We failed Brando because we didn't dramatise that nearly well enough.' It is not often that a director speaks of failing an actor, but it is a common occurrence and one to which Brando was becoming accustomed.

The Chase was a failure, with Pauline Kael speaking for many when she described it as a 'liberal sadomasochistic fantasy' (a reference to the severe beating that Brando's character receives at the hands of Val Rogers' lieutenants, itself a hangover from the 'martyr' period of Brando's career). But it is interesting to watch, it has a first-rate cast and it has improved with age.

Many of the spy movies that were released in 1965 could be described as 'conservative sadomasochistic fantasies', but they were certainly more popular with the audiences of the time. One such success was *The Ipcress File* starring Michael Caine and directed in England by a Canadian, Sidney J. Furie. Brando, bowing to financial pressure, accepted Universal's offer to star in Furie's first Hollywood assignment, an inept western, *The Appaloosa* (known as *South West to Sonora* in Britain). With its Mexican border setting and revenge theme, this might appear to be a return to the territory of *One-Eyed Jacks* but it holds none of that film's interest. In fact, it holds very little interest at all and Brando is clearly bored in his role as a buffalo hunter whose most prized possession is the appaloosa horse of the title. John Saxon, who is very entertaining as the film's villain, summed up the plot as 'boy meets horse, boy loses horse, boy gets horse'. *The Ipcress File* had been marked by Furie's singular choice of camera angles which gave the film a modish look – now horribly dated. To Brando's dismay, Furie was intent on employing the same quirky set-ups on *The Appaloosa*.

One member of the crew is said to have remarked: 'Furie's even shooting up the horse's ass', which may be apocryphal but neatly sums up the public and critical reaction to the film.

If the failure of *The Appaloosa* served to confirm – for some – the continuing decline of Marlon Brando, there was worse to come. In January 1966, Brando flew into London to begin work on a film that would be directed by one of his childhood heroes, a man who bore one of the most famous names in cinema – (indeed, he was once considered the most famous man in the world): Charlie Chaplin. Their collaboration would bring one man's career to an inglorious close, and pull the other's down to a level from which he would have to fight hard to recover.

Brando as Matt Fletcher, bent on revenge in The Appaloosa. *Co-star John Saxon summed up the film as: 'boy meets horse, boy loses horse, boy gets horse'.*

9

A catalogue of misfortune

Brando with Sophia Loren in Charlie Chaplin's ill-starred A Countess from Hong Kong *(above). Brando as Peter Quint (right) in* The Nightcomers, *Michael Winner's 'prequel' to* The Turn of the Screw.

IT MUST have seemed like a good idea at the time. After all, the notion of bringing together two cinematic legends – each of whom had been called a genius at one time or another – was sure to excite a great deal of public interest. But then again, Chaplin directing Brando? It is hard to imagine why one of the world's greatest comedians should have chosen – as the star of his last feature film – a man who possessed all the comic sophistication of a whoopee cushion.

The genesis of *A Countess from Hong Kong* dated from a trip Chaplin made to Shanghai in 1931. A few years later, he conceived a romantic comedy set in the Chinese port as a vehicle for Paulette Goddard who was living with him as his wife. In Chaplin's original story, Goddard would play a Russian countess who had fallen on hard times and was forced to earn a living from prostitution. Pursued by the police, she stows away on a ship where she meets a stuffy American millionaire (to be played by Gary Cooper) who eventually falls in love with her and abandons plans to re-marry his ex-wife in favour of making an 'honest woman' of the countess. When Chaplin separated from Goddard, he dropped all plans to make the film, but the screenplay re-surfaced thirty years later at the instigation of the producer Jerome Epstein, a friend and associate of Chaplin's sons.

The story still had a certain charm, even if its content was considerably less risqué in the climate of the sixties. An even greater problem was that stars of the stature of Goddard and Cooper were in short supply. Cary Grant might have seemed a natural choice but he was close to retiring and was beginning to feel a little foolish playing romantic leads at the age of sixty-two.

Given the limitation of choice, Chaplin seems to have sought out what he saw as the modern equivalent of Cooper – a masculine type

who combined authority with sex appeal. Brando was certainly that. Chaplin had gone on record as an admirer of Brando's work even if he had some difficulty remembering Brando's name (a problem which, some sources claim, continued on the set of *Countess*).

The plot of the new film remained virtually unchanged from Chaplin's original idea, with Brando cast as Ogden Mears, a millionaire diplomat en route by luxury liner from Hong Kong to San Francisco. For the stowaway Countess herself, Chaplin decided on Sophia Loren, whose work he had enjoyed in the Italian film *Yesterday, Today and Tomorrow*. Loren may have lacked the earthiness of Magnani or the good humour of Gina Lollobrigida, but she had proved herself an able comedienne opposite Cary Grant in *Houseboat*, and she was exceptionally beautiful.

The supporting cast included Tippi Hedren (the uninteresting blonde who had starred in two of Hitchcock's most recent, and least interesting, films), Chaplin's son, Sydney, and two British actors of undoubted comic talent: Margaret Rutherford and Patrick Cargill. But it was the supposedly magical combination of Chaplin, Brando and Loren that was intended to sell the film: how could it go wrong?

Well, in the first place, there was Brando's obvious unsuitability for his role. When Bette Davis was filming *Elizabeth and Essex* and saw Errol Flynn approaching her in one of their scenes, she is said to have wished it was Laurence Olivier. So it is with Brando as Ogden Mears. Every time he enters a scene you wish it was Cary Grant. What made things worse for Brando was that Chaplin insisted on acting out every piece of direction and manipulated the actors right down to the finest details of a performance. Brando had previously worked like that to some extent with Kazan. But he had trusted Kazan; with Chaplin he had not the slightest rapport.

Such was Chaplin's status as a screen legend that the set became an attraction for a variety of visitors – among them François Truffaut and John Huston – all keen to pay homage to the great man. But Chaplin's greatness was a thing of the past. The filming of *A Countess from Hong Kong* was an unhappy experience for most of those involved. Brando, full of respect for his director's body of work, indulged Chaplin but was unable to tailor his approach to the demands of a lamentably weak script. He had been ill-advised to accept the role but, as he told Associated Press reporter Bob Thomas: 'When a man of his stature in the industry writes a script for you, you can hardly refuse. Why he should think of me for a comedy, I haven't the faintest idea.'

There was little or no spark between Brando and Loren, which killed the last hope of any life in the film. The comic highlights, if they can be called that, came from Cargill, Rutherford and – in a tiny role as a seasick steward – Chaplin himself. By all accounts, Chaplin believed

'Chaplin insisted on acting out every piece of direction...'. Chaplin directs Brando and Loren in A Countess from Hong Kong.

he was making a great film and he continued to think so even after the critics had given it a unanimous panning. Chaplin was loved but only in cherished memory – all the love in the world could not save his last film from being quickly consigned to oblivion.

The misfortune that had dogged Brando since *Mutiny on the Bounty* had had a damaging effect on his position as a 'bankable commodity', a term which he might find distasteful but which nevertheless determined the quality of the work he was offered. By 1967, he was no longer anyone's first choice for leading roles in Hollywood and he looked set to follow a number of lesser actors into lending an American name to a cheaply-made European movie of the sort that reached its commercial peak with Sergio Leone's 'Spaghetti Westerns'.

Press coverage of his private life centred on the often bitter legal battles between Brando and Anna Kashfi over custody of their son, Christian. That, and speculation about his current romantic involvement, were all that interested the media. There was, for example, very little intelligent response to his activity on behalf of the Civil Rights movement. Throughout the 1960s Brando was a familiar figure at Civil Rights events – shortly after the completion of the Chaplin film, he had joined Sammy Davis Jnr. and Burt Lancaster at a march and rally in Mississippi. His growing interest in the history and present living conditions of North American Indians was treated by the press as proof of his continued eccentricity. Such social concerns were not the expected province of Hollywood film stars and Brando's motives were suspect –

his liberal conscience was often seen as a means of gaining publicity at a time when his career was at a low ebb. In fact, his tireless concern for the problems faced by minorities in American society was genuine and would cost him dearly in terms of personal popularity as well as financial commitment. Other actors espoused political causes without damaging their popularity: Paul Newman for one. Ironically, Newman had started his career with a barrage of criticism for his mimicry of Brando; now he was the natural choice for directors and producers in search of the quality that Brando had first brought to Hollywood.

Another star whose prominence was greater than Brando's at this time was Steve McQueen and he had originally been cast to co-star with Newman in the forthcoming *Butch Cassidy and the Sundance Kid*. When a proposal was made to switch the lead roles so that Newman would be playing Cassidy and McQueen the Sundance Kid, McQueen bowed out of the project. Newman and director George Roy Hill then decided that Brando would be an ideal replacement but they were unable to locate him. It is quite possible that Brando's unhappy experience of Westerns – added to the popular belief that the genre had played itself out – led him to give Newman's film a wide berth. As it turned out, the film was an enormous success of the sort that Brando needed but at the time, seemed fated never to have again. It also made a star of the young man who eventually played the Sundance Kid, an actor who had only recently had a supporting role in a Brando film, Robert Redford.

As Brando's career continued its downward spiral, that of his one-time rival Montgomery Clift came to a sudden and tragic halt. Clift had been in poor shape since his car accident but he had managed to turn out a half dozen strong performances in the years that followed. One of these, in 1960, was for Brando's old mentor Elia Kazan, who chose Clift to replace an unavailable Brando in *Wild River*. Kazan observed that Clift was 'a tenderhearted shell of a man' and was impressed by the actor's control of his serious drinking problem during shooting. 'I knew I was handling a sick man,' Kazan has written, 'who was goodhearted and in no way evil.' Sick he may have been, but Clift was doing the kind of work that was eluding the perfectly healthy Brando.

The two other notable films at the end of Clift's career were both directed by John Huston – not a man who might readily be associated with such a sensitive actor. Huston was always at his best directing the action pictures which suited his temperament, but he had a literary side to his nature which drew him to adaptations of novels such as *Moby Dick* and *Under the Volcano*, but the results were almost always crude approximations of the original.

Clift worked with Huston for the last time in the title role of *Freud* (from a screenplay by Jean-Paul Sartre). The result was an unhappy experience for everyone concerned but it did not prevent Huston from considering Clift for the male lead in his adaptation of Carson McCullers' novel, *Reflections in a Golden Eye*. Elizabeth Taylor, Clift's closest Hollywood friend, had originated the project as a vehicle for herself and she was adamant that Clift was the best choice to co-star. Her arguments swayed the reluctant Huston who had found Clift's personal problems an intolerable strain on their working relationship in *Freud*. Unlike Brando, Clift's chief drawback was not his unbankability but his poor health which made him virtually uninsurable for a major film part. Partly to see if he could stand up to the strain, Warner Brothers-Seven Arts (the production company for *Reflections*) agreed to cast Clift in a lamentable spy picture called *The Defector*. It was a difficult experience for Clift who had been absent from the screen for four years, but he forced himself through it. Whether or not Warners and Huston were convinced by his effort is debatable, but the point is academic. Barely two months after completing *The Defector*, Montgomery Clift suffered a fatal heart attack.

Dean, Clift and Brando were the three great acting hopes of fifties Hollywood. Now two were dead, and the third appeared to be a spent force. But, like a gladiator picking up the sword of a fallen comrade, Brando stepped in to replace Clift and *Reflections in a Golden Eye* gave him his one moment of glory in a decade of failure.

After Clift's death, Elizabeth Taylor and John Huston considered a number of actors before deciding on Marlon Brando. Brando himself was uncertain that he was entirely suitable for the role of Major Weldon Penderton, a latent homosexual married to a beautiful wife, Leonora (played by Taylor) but harbouring a secret desire for a young soldier (Robert Forster) on a U.S. Army post in Georgia. This subject matter had been a reason for more than one star declining the role and had convinced Taylor that Clift would be ideally cast.

In fact, Brando – with his burly physique and authoritarian bearing – makes Penderton a more complex character than he might have been if portrayed by the more overtly sensitive Clift. It makes greater dramatic sense to have this bullish martinet repressing his sexuality and revealing himself through sudden moments of fear and hesitation. Brando's subtle performance presents us with a tormented man hiding a progressively thinner veneer of bluff masculinity.

John Huston invited Brando to St. Clerans, Huston's home in Ireland to discuss the film. Various screen treatments had been prepared, including versions by Francis Ford Coppola and Christopher Isherwood, before Huston settled on a Scottish novelist, Chapman Mortimer, to write the final script. It was still being typed up as Huston and Brando talked about the role of Penderton. Brando expressed his doubts to Huston who suggested that he wait until the script was ready before coming to a decision. After reading the script Brando walked out of

Brando as Major Penderton kills the object of his repressed desire in Reflections in a Golden Eye.

131

the house and into a fierce rainstorm. 'When he came back,' Huston recalled, 'he said simply, "I want to do it".'

In his autobiography *An Open Book*, Huston makes only a passing reference to Brando's acting technique. In the course of their first conversation Huston had asked Brando if he could ride a horse. Brando replied that 'he had been raised on a horse ranch.' When they were shooting the film, Huston noticed that Brando 'exhibited such a fear of horses that presently Elizabeth Taylor, who is a good horsewoman, began to be afraid also. I wondered then, as now, if Marlon got this fear because he had so immersed himself in his role. The character he played had a fear of horses. It could well be.'

Elizabeth Taylor had planned to have her husband Richard Burton for the role of Leonora's lover, Colonel Langdon, but he lost interest in the project. In the event the part was played by Brian Keith (by no means as big a star as Burton, but a much better screen actor) with Julie Harris as his wife, who takes platonic comfort from their houseboy, played by a New York hairdresser, Zorro David. To round off this tangled web of relationships, Private Williams – the object of Major Penderton's covert interest – is himself fixated with Leonora.

McCullers' gallery of grotesques has a certain kinship with those of Tennessee Williams but whereas Williams used dramatic images and lyrical dialogue to define his characters, Carson McCullers operated in the more intimate world of the novelist. Removed from their proper medium of the stage or the printed page, the works of both these writers could often appear absurd and overheated. Huston chose to ignore the peculiarities of the characters and concentrate instead on the psychological aspects of the story. The actors were discouraged from merely 'presenting' their characters, as had been the case in Huston's previous film with Stark, a self-consciously 'steamy' version of Tennessee Williams' *Night of the Iguana*, and the result was a group of tightly contained performances of which Brando's was particularly effective.

Brando invests Penderton with scores of tiny mannerisms and reactions which combine to chart the decline of a disturbed personality. His reaction when his horse throws him is a brilliant study of a proud man's humiliation. Alternately laughing and crying, his almost childlike distress is palpable as he beats the horse. When he is himself whipped by his wife the image does not connect at all with 'Brando the martyr' of earlier films. This is Brando as a man who uses his personal arrogance as a mask, a man for whom a uniform – and the rank which it denotes – cannot prevent the final, painful exposure of his own violent weaknesses. It is Brando's one major performance from the sixties but it came at the wrong time in the wrong film.

Taylor cannot match Brando's power in the film. She plays Leonora as a glamourised variation on the ball-breaking vulgarian from *Who's*

Brando's performance as the repressed army officer (shown here with his wife played by Elizabeth Taylor) in Reflections in a Golden Eye *was his best in some time — and the only real showing of his talent during the sixties.*

Afraid of Virginia Woolf? Robert Forster was little more than a cipher as Private Williams and Zorro David was encouraged to camp up his role as the houseboy. Huston might be praised for taking on such a difficult subject but he was depicting a negative portrait of homosexual desire and his treatment of it was often crudely mismanaged. Only Brian Keith (here playing one of the few roles that have been commensurate with his talent) and Julie Harris came close to Brando.

Huston took a great deal of trouble over the look of the film, that is to say he had the Technicolor stock processed in a way that would suffuse the film with a golden glow. He was fond of experimenting with colour in this way; he had processed the colour stock on *Moby Dick* with black-and-white chemicals to give the film the look of old whaling prints, and his biographical portrait of Toulouse-Lautrec, *Moulin Rouge*, had tried to capture the bold colour used by the Parisian impressionist painter. As with those earlier experiments, the studio took a different view and *Reflections in a Golden Eye* was released in a standard colour print. Nevertheless, Huston classed the film among his best work. In his autobiography he wrote: 'Scene by scene – in my humble estimation – it is pretty hard to fault.'

Brando and Huston worked well together and admired each other's work, but Brando was far from the hard-drinking macho types that formed the director's inner circle of male friends. He was at his professional best on the set, giving Huston no cause to indulge his supposed excesses. Huston did however indulge Elizabeth Taylor, who frequently arrived late on the set, often surrounded by her personal entourage. 'Elizabeth took a long time over her make-up,' Huston recalled, without rancour. 'I understood this. It was part of her professionalism. She would not appear in front of a camera other than at her best.' Be that as it may, Taylor still had a formidable reputation to live down – akin to Brando's after *Bounty* – arising from her behaviour on the set of *Cleopatra*. But whereas Brando had found himself cold-shouldered by Hollywood, Taylor's power had increased. *Reflections in a Golden Eye* was not a Brando picture – it was not even a Huston picture – it was an Elizabeth Taylor picture, and that was how the filmgoing public were going to receive it.

The public did not like it; Liz could be better than this (that is to say, she could be more glamorous) and Brando was no substitute for Burton. (Nobody even considered Brian Keith, he wasn't a star.) The critics, on the other hand, were considerably warmer and were pleased to find Brando back on form. But, without a popular following, the film was destined to have a short life and Brando's impact was too little, too late.

For Brando himself, the public apathy which greeted the release of *Reflections* could only have confirmed his disenchantment with film acting. He was constantly reminded of the actor's unimportance in relation to the more serious things that were going on in the world. America was going through a violent period in its history with political assassinations at home and a futile war overseas. Immediately before he played Penderton, Brando had travelled to India to see for himself the terrible effects of famine in the Bihar region. He described it as 'a baptism of fire' and involved himself in fund-raising activities for UNICEF. In an interview with UNICEF's Jacques Danois, he said: 'I have seen ugliness beyond describing...children covered with sores from head to foot. It is time to realise that if we don't care for all peoples, irrespective of their colour and political disposition...then there is a very good expectation that we simply won't survive as a species.'

Much of *Reflections* was shot in Italy, Brando would spend the next few years working outside Hollywood, in films that reflected the obscurity he was sliding into. Although Europe was the main source of his employment, it was not in the kind of European films that had attracted him in the 'fifties.

The first of them was *Candy*, directed by Brando's old friend, Christian Marquand. Marquand was the French actor after whom Brando named his son by Anna Kashfi – and whom Kashfi inferred was sexually interested in her husband. Whatever the truth of the Brando-Marquand relationship, Brando felt fond enough of his old friend to help him get funding for his second directorial venture by accepting the cameo role of an Indian guru.

Brando on stage in 1967 in a Tahitian dance routine as part of a UNICEF gala in Paris.

Candy was based on a satirical novel (a semi-pornographic variation of Voltaire's *Candide*) by Terry Southern and Mason Hoffenberg. The book had enjoyed a growing underground reputation since its appearance ten years before but, even in 1968, its content was considered too explicit for any major studio to back a film version. Brando's commitment to the project opened the door for Marquand to secure the services of Richard Burton, Charles Aznavour and James Coburn for what would prove to be one of many films of that period whose studied 'permissiveness' was horribly dated even at the moment of their release. This fiasco fed the suspicion that *Reflections in a Golden Eye* was now the exception rather than the rule for Brando, and his next film confirmed his diminished status.

According to Pauline Kael, Brando was never 'worse or less interesting' than in *The Night of the Following Day*, the last of his films for Universal, completing the five-picture deal he signed with the studio at the time of *The Ugly American*. This mediocre attempt at a thriller centred on the kidnapping of a young heiress (played by Pamela Franklin) by a gang of kidnappers led by the sadistic Leer (Richard Boone) and including an inarticulate chauffeur (Brando in a blond wig). It is a mess of a film, often looking like a witless pastiche of the French New Wave thrillers – themselves knowing pastiches of Hollywood movies – made by Jean-Luc Godard and François Truffaut, the kidnappers are American, the girl is English and her rich father is French, as is the location. The production was originated – under the aegis of Elliot Kastner – by Hubert Cornfield. Cornfield had earned a reputation as a director of 'interesting' films – that is to say, low-budget commercial failures that had attracted a measure of critical acclaim – like *Plunder Road* and *Pressure Point*. With Robert Phippeney, he scripted *The Night of the Following Day* from *The Snatchers*, a novel by Lionel White, whose work had formed the basis for Stanley Kubrick's *The Killing* and Godard's *Pierrot le Fou*. Cornfield envisaged the French star Yves Montand in the leading role but when Montand's previous commitments made him unavailable, Richard Boone was brought in to take over. Boone – best known to the general public for his role as Paladin, the sardonic hired gunman in the TV series *Have Gun, Will Travel* – stepped down to a supporting role when Brando was contracted via Jay Kanter, now Universal's British production head. Boone had known Brando at the Actors Studio and the two men worked happily together; so much so that, when Brando began arguing with Cornfield over the interpretation of his role, he insisted that Boone took over the direction. Perhaps with Montand and Nicole Courcel (the French actress who was Cornfield's original choice for the role of the chauffeur's wife), it might have been nearer to the film that Cornfield had set out to make. After Brando was cast, Courcel was dropped in favour of Rita Moreno whose career had not matched the promise suggested by the

Brando at his lowest ebb – as the guru Grindl in Christian Marquand's Candy.

Best Supporting Actress Oscar she won for *West Side Story* in 1962. Moreno had had a stormy love affair with Brando before his marriage to Anna Kashfi. Unable to revive their romance after Brando's divorce from Kashfi, Moreno attempted suicide and later underwent lengthy psychiatric treatment. Despite all this, she and Brando were reconciled as friends and it was at his suggestion that she was cast opposite him in *The Night of the Following Day*. However, whatever rapport Brando may have had with his co-stars, it did not extend to his director. In any event, Cornfield had little or no rapport with his actors. 'Working with Marlon *sucked*,' said Cornfield, who fared little better with Boone. Responding to one piece of direction, Boone remarked: 'Okay, Hubert, I'll do it. But it makes about as much sense to me as a rat fucking a grapefruit.'

The unhappy result of this ill-starred collaboration was given poor distribution and was universally panned by those critics who bothered to review it. Brando's name, once a guarantee of quality, had become a by-word for trash – worse, for dull trash.

The cumulative effect of *Candy* and *The Night of the Following Day* would not be felt until the end of 1968, well after Brando had completed them, and by then Elia Kazan would have made a brief re-appearance in Brando's life and something far more significant would have happened to take him away from the cinema.

Despite the success of *On the Waterfront*, Brando and Kazan had been estranged for many years. Kazan believed this to be the result of their political differences but it may just as easily have been that Brando wanted to prove that he did not need Kazan to make him a remarkable actor. Several critics of Brando's films in the sixties took pains to note that he was at his best under Kazan's direction. Kazan himself (in an autobiography that crawls with vanity, leavened by a false modesty that makes little effort to disguise itself) has written of his attempt to cast Brando in his 1968 film, *The Arrangement* and thus 'bring him back from some bad outings'. He quotes a letter he wrote to Brando in which he asked the actor to lose some of the weight he had gained in recent years to play the leading role of Eddie Anderson, a middle-aged advertising man who has betrayed the artistic ambitions of his youth. The letter ends: 'I want you to do this film but I only want you if you're genuinely enthusiastic about it and only if you will come to me ten months from now at the weight you were at during *On the Waterfront*. Be a true friend and don't kid me. If you really want to, you can be a blazing actor again. The wanting is the hard part. Much love. E.K.'

The implication, that Kazan – and only Kazan – could make Brando 'a blazing actor again' is reinforced in other parts of the letter which dismiss the Chaplin film and praise Brando's performance in *Reflections* as one given 'without any real help from Huston'.

Brando as the chauffeur in The Night of the Following Day.

The letter – which may have been edited for the autobiography but certainly reads as if it was written with an eye on publication – contains those elements in Kazan's writing (his ostentatious directness, his relentless self-justification and his all-embracing grandiosity) which make him seem distinctly creepy. On the very first page of his book, Kazan writes: 'Confronting me where I'm sitting at my typewriter is a small round mirror, clamped in a pretty but rickety Mex-made stand. It frames my face neatly, and sometimes when I work, I study my image.' This vanity vitiates the professed honesty of the book and infects Kazan's judgement of his contemporaries – including Brando.

Brando began to show a real interest in *The Arrangement* and there is no doubt that the proposition of his working with Kazan again excited the Hollywood community. At one point, Brando met with Kazan to discuss the hairpieces he would need for the role. In retrospect, Kazan told one interviewer that Brando may have found the character of Eddie 'uncomfortable. It was very, very close to something basic in him.' It was obvious that some commentators would draw parallels between the ad-man who was a defeated writer and the film star who was a defeated actor. 'All Marlon had to do was come and be photographed' Kazan wrote later. 'You could have read the part on his face. Talk about typecasting!' But 1968 was a year of political upheaval which saw the assassinations in America of Martin Luther King and Robert Kennedy. Both deaths had a profound effect on Brando whose commitment to the Civil Rights movement now held greater importance for him than his work in the cinema. On hearing of King's death, he invited Kazan to his house and explained that he could not now go on with *The Arrangement*; he was too overwhelmed by the tragedy of King's death and its implications for America. As Kazan drove away from Brando's home, he caught sight of the actor in his rear-view mirror: 'he looked desolate,' Kazan recalled, 'I never saw Marlon again, haven't seen him to this day.'

Although Kazan accepted Brando's reasons for abandoning the film, he very quickly had second thoughts: 'It was a few hours before I remembered that he was one hell of an actor, and although his feeling about King was certainly sincere, the depth of emotion he projected came as much from his talent as from his sense of tragedy. Then I began to get mad. We were already making the man's hairpieces, for chrissake!' Hell hath no fury…

One week after the King assassination, Bobby Hutton, a 17-year-old member of the Black Panther movement, was killed by police in Oakland, California. Bobby Seale, the Panthers' leader in the area, claimed that Hutton had already surrendered and been told to run to a police car when he was shot ten times. Brando attended Hutton's funeral and a large rally protesting at the arrest of another Panther, Huey Newton, on charges of killing a policeman. At the rally, Brando addressed the assembled crowd: 'I have just come from the funeral of Bobby Hutton...that could have been my son lying there. The preacher said the white man can't cool it because he never dug it. That is why I am here.' Brando had been to inspect the scene of Hutton's death and was convinced that the police contention – that they told Hutton to stop and he ignored them – was a lie. 'You've been listening four hundred years to white people and they haven't done a thing.' He told the Newton rally, 'I'm going to begin right now informing white people what they don't know.'

He was as good as his word, appearing on talk shows to present the Black Panthers' version of the Hutton killing and telling Johnny Carson that he was donating one per cent of his income to Martin Luther King's Southern Christian Leadership Conference. Other stars, he said, would be doing the same – and he instanced Paul Newman and Barbra Streisand. Carson immediately announced that he would be following suit. Brando made it clear that he was no longer interested in acting except in films of 'appropriate significance' and he increased his financial commitment to the Civil Rights cause to 12 per cent. It was at this time that he was asked to appear with Newman in *Butch Cassidy and the Sundance Kid* but this did not attract him. What did attract him was an offer from the Italian director Gillo Pontecorvo, whose film, *The Battle of Algiers* had been a potent example of politicised cinema.

Brando as the Englishman Sir William Walker in Queimada! *(top). Brando on the set of* Queimada! *(above). Cast and crew spent seven months filming in Colombia, South America, with the rest of the film shot in North Africa.*

Pontecorvo was preparing a film which would attack Western colonialism in the nineteenth century while drawing clear parallels with the modern world. Brando was approached to play Sir William Walker, a British diplomat who arrives on the Caribbean island of Queimada to incite a revolution, thus breaking the Portuguese control of the sugar-cane industry, enabling it to fall into the hands of the British. The islanders themselves would, of course, be mere pawns in the power game between the imperial nations.

The name 'Queimada' means 'burn' in Portuguese, providing an ironic sub-text to the story. Pontecorvo was inspired to make his film when he heard of a Caribbean island which had been put to the torch in 1520 by Spaniards who were intent on quelling a native rebellion there. Black slaves were then transported to the burnt-out island which was re-named Quemada, the Spanish spelling for the word for 'burn'. The Spanish government, still in the grip of the Franco dictatorship, objected to the title, claiming that the film would reflect badly on the country's colonial history, and threats were made to impose an official ban on the film's release. A previous ban had not only affected Fred Zinnemann's *Behold a Pale Horse*, based on a Spanish Civil War story by Emeric Pressburger, but had been extended for years afterward to all films produced by the production company, Columbia. As Portugal was a less important market without the wider influence of Spain, the spelling of the title was changed to the Portuguese version and the story was amended accordingly. This compromise, governed as it was by commercial interests, was hardly a propitious beginning for the project.

Pontecorvo worked on his initial idea with Franco Solinas and Giorgio Arlorio, who prepared the final script which was submitted to Brando. Brando liked it, and Pontecorvo then brought in the Italian producer Alberto Grimaldi who had secured the American distributors United Artists for his previous productions, the Clint Eastwood 'Spaghetti Westerns'. Grimaldi's success with the Eastwood films assuaged UA's objections to Brando, and *Queimada* began filming in Cartagena, Colombia, in late 1968.

The company remained in Colombia for seven months, during which time relations between Brando and Pontecorvo became strained, to say the least. Pontecorvo was unused to working with star actors. The methods he had used with the unknowns who made up the cast of *The Battle of Algiers* simply did not work with Brando. More seriously, Pontecorvo's manner seemed at odds with the noble intentions of the film itself. He underpaid black extras and mistreated the horses on location. Many company members fell ill, including a young boy who was forced to go on working by the increasingly dictatorial director. The unyielding heat made for appalling working conditions and Brando finally rebelled on everyone's behalf, insisting that the

Brando with extras on the set of Queimada!

company be relocated or, he said, he would quit.

With only ten days filming left, Grimaldi moved the unit to Marrakesh but the situation between Brando and his director was no easier. 'Right now I want to kill Gillo,' Brando told a visiting journalist, 'I really want to kill him...he has no fucking feeling for people.' Pontecorvo, on the other hand, maintained that Brando was 'a great artist...But – I never saw an actor before who was so afraid of the camera...Brando is also a little – how you say? – paranoiac. He thinks when I make forty takes it's because I want to break him. Why should I want to break him?'

With the film completed, Grimaldi filed a lawsuit against Brando alleging unreasonable behaviour on the set. No doubt he was disappointed that his faith in Brando had resulted in a film that was obviously doomed to failure. The title had to be translated for the North American audience, who were not expected to understand it, and the film was released there as *Burn!*

If *Queimada* was a disaster for Brando, it was even worse for Pontecorvo who has worked little since. Brando is interesting as Walker (reprising his Fletcher Christian accent to some extent) but the storyline is confused and reflects the spirit of compromise in which the film was conceived. Most critics were beyond disappointment where Brando was concerned. The release of *Queimada* in 1970 confirmed the general opinion that Marlon Brando was washed up at the early age of 46.

That year Brando came to England to star in *The Nightcomers*, an uninspired 'prequel' to Henry James' celebrated ghost story, *The Turn of the Screw*. The James story had been filmed (as *The Innocents*) by Jack Clayton in 1962 with Deborah Kerr as the new governess haunted by the spirits of the previous governess, Miss Jessel and her lover, the game-keeper Peter Quint, glimpsed briefly in Clayton's film in the person of Peter Wyngarde. *The Nightcomers* set out to tell the horrific tale that James only hinted at in his original, with Stephanie Beacham starring as Miss Jessel opposite Brando's Quint. The director was Michael Winner, an ambitious young man who had earlier secured the services of another Hollywood outcast, Orson Welles, for his comedy *I'll Never Forget Whatsisname*. Winner approached Brando through Jay Kanter (who had left Universal and gone into partnership with Elliott Kastner). The film was shot in six weeks – Winner is never less than workmanlike – which must have been a relief to Brando after the lengthy location work on *Queimada*. With more subtle direction, it might have amounted to an interesting venture but Winner is incapable of giving anything other than a surface reading of his material. His greatest success lay ahead with the dreadful *Death Wish* series of films starring Charles Bronson. For *The Nightcomers* he rehearsed his now-familiar obsession with gratuitous sexual violence in the sado-masochistic relationship between Quint and Miss Jessel.

Brando with his 'favourite director' Michael Winner on the set of The Nightcomers.

Brando's name was so insignificant in box office terms that *The Nightcomers* failed to secure a British release until some time after it was made. It might not have been released at all in its country of origin had not Brando's next film – work on which he delayed for Winner's benefit – been the kind of international success which had long since eluded him.

Paramount Pictures, the studio which would next employ Brando, had lost a great deal of money on *The Brotherhood*, a film about the Mafia starring Kirk Douglas. They were less than enthusiastic therefore when they found they had bought the rights to Mario Puzo's best-selling book on the same theme. As far as Paramount were concerned, the Puzo book could be turned into a low-budget movie which could be safely entrusted to a fairly new director, Francis Ford Coppola, whose films were less than box-office winners, but who had won an Academy Award for his screenplay of *Patton*. The studio rationalised that a modest budget of $2 million could be expended on the project that also promised a good role for the actor who had played the title role in *Patton* (and also won an Oscar in the process), George C. Scott. The only problem was the memory of their experience with *The Brotherhood*. Would they get their fingers burnt again with this new film – with a similarly familial title? *The Godfather*?

Brando as Quint engages in sexual sadism with Stephanie Beacham as Miss Jessel in The Nightcomers.

10

Success is the best revenge

Don Vito Corleone (Brando) dances with his daughter (Coppola's sister Talia Shire) on her wedding day in The Godfather *(above). Brando's performance as Don Corleone (right) resurrected his career in the early seventies.*

IN 1971, Francis Ford Coppola's track record as a director consisted of only three films: *You're a Big Boy Now, Finian's Rainbow* and *The Rain People*– none of which had made a big impression on critics or audiences. However, the Academy Award he received for the screenplay of *Patton* suggested that he was worthy of more attention and Paramount decided to entrust him with the direction of *The Godfather* (a project which had already been turned down by Richard Brooks and Costa-Gavras). Coppola was himself less than enthusiastic, especially when the studio made it clear that they wished to minimise the risk by giving the story a contemporary setting in keeping with the modest budget.

A number of actors were suggested for the title role – George C. Scott (newly bankable after *Patton*), Rod Steiger, Ernest Borgnine and Charles Bronson. Coppola wanted none of these. He had only two actors in mind for the role of Don Vito Corleone – Laurence Olivier or Marlon Brando. Olivier declined on the grounds of the ill-health which had just brought his stage career to an abrupt halt. Brando was not even approached because Paramount wanted nothing to do with him. He had, in fact, been sent a copy of Puzo's original novel by the author himself but had not read it, explaining to Puzo that he knew no major studio would consider hiring him. Coppola persisted, not only in asking for Brando, but in trying to convince Paramount that the film could only be shot with the appropriate period background. The shadow of *The Brotherhood* still hung over the studio's negotiations but the situation changed slightly when it became clear that Puzo's novel was turning into a bigger seller than had originally been imagined. Puzo's deal with the studio gave him the right to script the film but Coppola decided to take a hand here

too and work with him on stripping the book's excesses down into a sharp and punchy screenplay. The result of their collaboration was despatched to Brando, who liked it.

The problem remained of how to convince Paramount that Brando would be the best choice for the role. The company's president, Stanley Jaffe, and its production chief, Robert Evans, were both firmly set against Brando – so much so that Al Ruddy bet Coppola $200 that he would not be able to talk them round. But Coppola – who had initially expressed his wish to cast only Italian-Americans in the film's leading roles – remained determined to have Brando as the Don. His impassioned pleading failed to move the company's executives until he made three final propositions: that Brando would take no salary, only a percentage of the film's profits, that he would put up a financial bond as guarantee against any disruptive behaviour, and that he would submit to a screen test for the role. With so many safeguards built in to the deal, Paramount relented and allowed Coppola to pursue Brando more closely. There was only one catch – Coppola had not discussed the matter of a screen test with Brando himself, and wasn't at all sure how he could ask an actor of his stature to agree to such a thing.

By now, Brando had read Puzo's book and responded favourably to what he saw as its social sub-text. Puzo, Brando contended, was making the point that the Mafia thrived because it operated in the

Brando with Salvatore Corsitto, who played the undertaker Bonasera in The Godfather.

best traditions of American big business. The old adage of 'what's good for business is good for America' allowed the organisation's excesses to be absorbed into the fabric of American life. With the actor so well-disposed to the subject matter and already beginning his character study of Don Vito Corleone, Coppola found a way round the problem of the screen-test. He would ask Brando to experiment with make-up and then record the result on film. Brando agreed and immediately began working on ideas with his personal make-up man, Phil Rhodes – a long-time associate and veteran of the ill-fated *Arms and the Man* tour of 1953. With help from Rhodes, Brando stuffed tissue paper into his cheeks to create jowls, darkened his hair (adding a pencil-thin moustache at Coppola's suggestion), and proceeded to age himself twenty years into a man in his sixties.

When Coppola visited Brando at home to photograph the make-up on video-tape and 16mm film, he brought with him the actor Salvatore Corsitto – who had already been cast in the film as the undertaker, Bonasera. At first, Coppola asked Brando merely to go through some everyday actions – picking up a telephone, for example – so that he could have a sense of how the make-up would work in the final version. Then he invited Corsitto into the room and encouraged the two actors to improvise a scene together. To Coppola's relief, Brando was happy to go along with this and he stayed in character to play the brief scene with Corsitto. Coppola had got his screen-test.

The short sequence was shown to Evans and Jaffe who immediately dropped their objections to Brando. More importantly, Brando's 'test' was well received by Charles Bluhdorn, the businessman whose Gulf and Western Corporation now owned Paramount, making him the studio's corporate head. Brando was released from his obligation to put up a financial bond but he was still required to work without salary (on a profit-share deal that allowed him a minimum return of $150,000 and protected the studio by fixing a maximum payment of $1,500,000).

With Brando secured, Coppola set about finding the rest of his cast. For the roles of Tom Hagen, the Don's legal counsellor, and Sonny Corleone, (the explosive eldest son) he chose two actors who had worked on his previous film, *The Rain People*: Robert Duvall and James Caan. Duvall had worked with Brando in *The Chase* and he had a growing reputation as a character actor based on his performances in films from *To Kill a Mockingbird* to *True Grit*. His best-known role at this point was that of Frank Burns in Robert Altman's *M.A.S.H.* but he was not regarded as a star. Neither was Caan, despite leading roles in *Rabbit, Run* and *Games* (Curtis Harrington's Hollywood re-working of the French thriller, *Les Diaboliques*). These choices were grudgingly approved by Paramount who wanted bigger names, but Coppola ran into trouble over his casting of Michael Corleone, the son who goes

Godfather Vito Corleone with his heir-apparent Michael (Al Pacino).

Coppola directs Brando and Al Pacino in The Godfather.

on to inherit the Godfather's empire. Coppola wanted Al Pacino, who had won awards for his theatre work but whose only film of any note was *Panic in Needle Park*, a downbeat story of drug addiction which had not had a wide release despite its selection for the Cannes Film Festival.

Pacino, a slight young man with sleepy-eyed good looks, seemed too ineffectual to Evans and Jaffe. He lacked the qualities they were looking for in the character. Coppola continued to push for Pacino but consented to test other actors for the role. None of them was acceptable but, rather than bringing the studio around to Coppola's way of seeing things, this only caused Paramount to have doubts about the director. Coppola's determination to shoot the film in period was another problem. There was even talk of replacing him as director, by – among other candidates – Elia Kazan. Finally, Robert Evans saw *Panic in Needle Park* and recognised Pacino's abilities. At the same time, the extraordinary commercial success of *The Godfather* novel led to an increase in the film's proposed budget – allowing for the necessary period reconstruction.

With hindsight, it is clear to see why Paramount's executives were so nervous about *The Godfather*. Their experience with *The Brotherhood* was proof that the gangster movie was not easy to revive; the only real star in the new film was Brando who was long past his peak and came fresh from an unbroken record of ten commercial flops; Coppola was hardly the hottest young director in town; and the producer, Albert Ruddy, had come from television – where he had created the war comedy series, *Hogan's Heroes* – having only one successful film, the low-budget *Little Fauss and Big Halsy* to his credit. When production finally began, in March 1971, the atmosphere was far from relaxed.

'The tensions on *The Godfather* were terrific,' Robert Duvall recalled. 'Paramount didn't trust Coppola so they hired a standby director to follow him in case he fucked up. The Mafiosi were putting the movie down but their very members were playing parts. Brando kept repeating that the head of the Mafia was no worse then the head of Dupont.' Indeed, pressure from Italian-American organisations forced the film-makers to strike all direct reference to the Mafia from the script.

As for 'the family's' participation in the filming, Brando laughingly recalled in his 1989 television interview with Connie Chung that it led to the 'greatest mistake of my professional career'. He was referring to the fact that several members of the Bofalino family – one of the most important Mafia 'clans' – were acting as extras in the elaborate wedding scene at the beginning of the film. Having completed shooting his scenes, Brando 'mooned' the guests – 'mooning' being the infantile practice of baring one's buttocks in public, to which Brando had been introduced by James Caan.

In the same interview Brando dismissed Chung's insistence that the younger actors on *The Godfather* looked up to Brando and saw him as 'a teacher'. 'How do you know that?' Brando asked her. 'I read it,' replied Chung. A cue for Brando to express disdain at Chung's faith in newspaper reports. 'All I know,' Brando said, 'is that Jimmy Caan is one of the funniest guys I ever met.' But Brando was being deliberately evasive. Of course, the other actors on the film looked up to him, as Coppola realised when he called the cast together for his preliminary Italian dinner before shooting. Some of them – Pacino in particular – had borrowed so much from Brando that the influence was obvious. Brando may never have intended to be influential, but it is disingenuous of him to deny that he has been.

Paramount executives who visited the set were disturbed by Brando's apparent inability to learn his lines. But by now the cue cards were part of Brando's technique. He was comfortable working from them and was able to rationalise it as a method of retaining the freshness of a scene. However, executives were pleased to see that Brando was using his position of 'father figure' as a unifying force on set, thus giving Coppola valuable support. Gradually, the studio's anxieties were assuaged. Coppola was given the extra money he needed to shoot in period and all doubts about Brando were forgotten.

'If the film had a fault,' Robert Duvall said, 'I think it was that Coppola was too soft – added to the fact that Brando never likes to show the seedy side of any character he plays.' Be that as it may, Coppola can take credit for being the first director to cast Brando symbolically as the icon he had become. It had happened in the past, of course, with other film stars. Directors have never been slow to make use of the 'image' as a shortcut to fixing a character in the audience's mind. In *North by Northwest*, Hitchcock had to establish the character of an urbane advertising man over a short period of screen time before plunging him into a breakneck story of espionage. Simply by casting Cary Grant, he saved himself and his screenwriter a great deal of trouble – the audience immediately identified the hero as the epitome of debonair urbanity.

Brando's mimetic talent allowed him to capture the gestures and demeanour of an elderly Italian-American. The Corleone voice – which would replace Terry Malloy's mumble in the impersonator's repertoire – was a strangled whisper inspired by the voice of the real-life gangster Frank Costello. The performance is a masterpiece of characterisation much subtler than his earlier attempts to submerge himself in characters like Zapata. With Don Vito Corleone, Brando succeeded in re-inventing his public image.

The performance is certainly mannered – as most of Brando's performances had become in recent years – but the mannerisms were held in check to serve the role. In one scene the sniffing of a flower – a gesture whose theatricality recalled Olivier's flower-sniffing in *Othello* – is a conceit of the character, not the actor. Once again, Brando's watchfulness is in evidence, but it is slower now, he is no longer seeking to understand but conferring his approval or disdain. Corleone is a figure of unquestioned power and it is the other actors who have to watch him. Terry Malloy has become Johnny Friendly – but Corleone is quieter, more secure than Friendly. Although there are many Hollywood actors who could have played the Don effectively, the character is on screen for little more than a third of the film's running time and he has to be a dominating presence. Brando's mythic importance particularly to younger actors provided this persuasive tension. It is hard to think of another actor who could have achieved that dominance even before he appeared on screen.

The Godfather would restore Brando's reputation and eclipse the failure of *The Nightcomers*. Of course, this has something to do with his acting – but not too much. The film outgrossed *Gone with the Wind* and *The Sound of Music*, making it the most successful Hollywood film to date. That is the kind of achievement Hollywood understands, and there were reviews to match. In *Newsweek*, Paul D. Zimmerman wrote: 'There is no longer any need to talk tragically of Marlon Brando's career. His stormy two-decade odyssey through films good and bad, but rarely big enough to house his prodigious talents, has ended in triumph...the king has returned to claim his throne.' The response from other influential critics like Pauline Kael in the *New Yorker* was just as enthusiastic, but the important news in Hollywood was that Brando was bringing in money again. He was back in the fold. Or so it seemed.

Shortly before the opening of *The Godfather*, Brando returned to Europe to work on the kind of film that had interested him at the very start of his career: a European 'art movie'. He had received another offer from Alberto Grimaldi (the producer of *Queimada!*), this time working with the Italian director Bernardo Bertolucci, whose film of Moravia's *The Conformist* Brando had seen and admired.

Bertolucci had originally planned his new film to star Jean-Louis Trintignant and Dominique Sanda (whose partnership had been so successful in *The Conformist*) but Sanda became pregnant and Trintignant expressed reservations about the planned sexual content

Brando with Italian director Bernardo Bertolucci on the set of Last Tango in Paris.

of the new project. Brando agreed to meet with Bertolucci and was sufficiently impressed to tell one journalist: '[Bertolucci] appeared to me as a man who is capable of extracting from an actor the best of himself and also of teaching him something. A man capable of doing something new, of tearing away all conventions, of overturning psychologies and renewing them, like a psychoanalyst.'

Brando agreed to replace Trintignant – with Sanda being replaced by Maria Schneider (an unknown actress who was incidentally the illegitimate daughter of the French star Daniel Gelin, one of Brando's friends). The film was to be called *Last Tango in Paris* and it was born of a male fantasy, a realm from which it never escaped.

'I have always longed to meet a woman in an empty apartment without knowing who that territory belonged to and to make love with her without knowing who she was.' said Bertolucci when asked about the inspiration of the film, 'I'd like to meet again and again without asking or being asked any questions.' That, more or less, is the basis of the relationship between the film's two central characters: Paul and Jeanne. There is a third character, Jeanne's fiancé a young film-maker played by Jean-Pierre Léaud, best known for his association with François Truffaut in the 'Antoine Doinel' series of films.

Like Coppola, Bertolucci was quick to make use of Brando's mythic stature. 'The two male characters are full of memories...' he said, 'Brando embodies physically and culturally the impact of American figures like Hemingway, Norman Mailer and Henry Miller in the same way that Léaud embodies my past as a cinéphile...' Throughout the filming, Bertolucci referred to Brando and Schneider as 'Marlon' and 'Maria', dropping all concern about their character names. 'From the beginning [Brando] was aware of the possibility of going beyond what is normally asked of him and what he can do with his eyes closed...I asked him to bring to the film all his experience as an actor and as a man. To become a Paul that was not synonymous with ceasing to be Brando. When I realised that Paul understood this I asked him to be Marlon, and not vice versa. At the end of the movie he told me: "I will never make a film like this one again. I don't like being an actor at the best of times but it's never been this bad. I felt violated from the beginning to the end, every day and at every moment. I felt that my whole life, my most intimate feelings and even my children had been torn from within me." '

Now that the controversy over its sexually explicit nature has died down, the only interesting thing about the film is Brando's performance. Bertolucci called *Last Tango* 'my very own *An American in Paris*' and, as a work of art, it suffers from the comparison.

The 'story' is an impoverished elaboration of Bertolucci's original fantasy: Paul, a run-down American who has failed in a variety of endeavours is coming to terms with the suicide of the wife who

Maria Schneider as Jeanne in Last Tango. *Schneider coped well with Brando's ad-libs but her role was little more than a cipher.*

Schneider and Brando in the empty apartment in Last Tango.

has cuckolded him. Jeanne, an amoral young French girl from a bourgeois background is hunting for the apartment where she will live with her fiancé after their marriage. Paul and Jeanne meet in the empty apartment, make love and go their separate ways. The meetings continue with Paul – who seems at first to be the dominant partner – finding his own rules of 'no names; no history' undermined by his growing obsession with Jeanne. When he pursues her through the streets of Paris and back to her own apartment he tells her that he loves her and asks her name. 'Jeanne' she tells him, and shoots him.

Discussing *Last Tango* in a 1979 *Playboy* interview, Brando said: 'I don't know *what* that film's about. So much of it was improvised. [Bertolucci] wanted to do this, to do that...He let me do anything. He told me the general area of what he wanted and I tried to produce the words or the action...I think it's all about Bernardo Bertolucci's psychoanalysis. And of his not being able to achieve...I don't know, I'm facetious...*he* didn't know what it was about, either.'

The best that can be said of *Last Tango* is that it is an exploration of the rage, frustration and fantasy world of the male menopause. Paul embodies many of the characteristics of the self-absorbed misogynist, ready to blame women for all his ills while seeking a cure from the same source. The allusions to Norman Mailer and Henry Miller are not accidental for the film contains many of their crude excesses.

It is easy to understand Brando's feeling of violation for, whereas Coppola used the actor symbolically, Bertolucci seemed intent on exploring the psychology of the Brando myth – albeit a myth which he had grafted on to his own obsession.

Brando looks very good in the film (Bertolucci encouraged him to lose weight) even though his eye make-up is rather too apparent. His performance is compelling – despite the limitations of the script – partly because few directors since Kazan had allowed the camera to linger so intently on the actor's face. But the mannerisms are there in full: the sudden body relaxation and thrown-back head which signals his incredulity; the finger stroking the eyebrow as he searches for a thought; the thrust-out jaw he uses for extra emphasis. Pauline Kael describes Paul as a 'self-pitying, self-dramatising clown' which just about gets it right – although Kael's contention that the first screening of *Last Tango in Paris* was an artistic landmark on a par with the première of Stravinsky's *Le Sacre du Printemps* is complete nonsense.

Last Tango is soft-core pornography for the carriage trade. Its much-vaunted shock value is based on scatalogically 'raunchy' dialogue and a few unconvincing sexual couplings. The whole thing is, in any case, undermined by the charmingly old-fashioned double standard which dictates that Maria Schneider should be photographed naked whenever possible, while Brando is allowed to stay fully dressed except for one nude scene of exemplary discretion. Having little to

Maria Schneider. Brando later dismissed Last Tango in Paris *but Schneider, whose subsequent career has been undistinguished, would refer to Bertolucci as her 'enemy'.*

*The 'Last Tango' in Paris
— Brando and Schneider.*

say about his characters, Bertolucci – like many a young film-maker – plunders film history for such irrelevancies as a glancing reference to Jean Vigo's masterpiece, *L'Atalante*: a life-preserver bearing the name of Vigo's famous barge is hurled into the Seine. There is also the casting of performers whose names have a certain resonance for 'cinéastes': Maria Michi from Rosselini's *Rome: Open City* as Paul's mother-in-law; Massimo Girotti, the hero of Visconti's *Ossessione* (an unauthorised version of *The Postman Always Rings Twice*) as the dead wife's lover; and Catherine Allegret, who bears a striking resemblance to her mother, Simone Signoret, makes a brief appearance as a maid. Add to this Bertolucci's iconographic use of Brando playing a character that we are encouraged to believe is virtually himself and it is easier to understand why some were fooled into thinking the film important.

Bertolucci's original script named the male character 'Leon' and gave him such portentous dialogue as: 'I make you die, you make me die, we're two murderers, each other's. But who succeeds in realising this is twice the murderer.' Not unreasonably, Brando jetisons all this and, by way of improvisation, builds a credible portrait of an emotionally crippled misogynist who has traded too long and too hard on his now-fading good looks. Sometimes affecting, as when Paul reminisces about his childhood on a farm (and Brando gives yet another version of his own upbringing); sometimes impressive as when he rages over the body of his dead wife: 'You cheap, goddam fucking Godforsaken whore...' then sobbingly apologises, Brando's

With Maria Schneider in
Last Tango.

performance ultimately counts for nothing because Bertolucci refuses to place it in any real context. As an exploration of the negative side of Brando's early 'seductive slob' image, it could have been fascinating but instead it just hangs in the air – never connecting with anything, least of all Maria Schneider's Jeanne. She, after all, is nothing more than the indiscreet object of his desire, the bitch-madonna-whore of a thousand masturbatory delusions. If only she had been drawn with more vigour and reality, Jeanne might have earned a round of applause for shooting this vainglorious jerk. For, in reality, monsters like Paul survive and stumble on to drag more women into the vortex of their self-regarding pain. Not that Bertolucci is really interested in showing a woman rejecting the role of victim. He simply has one last, enduring image for the cinéastes: before he falls mortally wounded on the balcony of Jeanne's apartment, Paul parks his chewing-gum – or rather Terry Malloy's chewing-gum, Stanley Kowalski's chewing-gum – on the balcony wall. The great sexual animal has finally been lured to his death and martyred in his moment of greatest weakness – declaring his love. The symbolism is grindingly obvious.

To watch Brando in *On the Waterfront* and then in *Last Tango in Paris* is to see a remarkable naturalistic actor at work and it is impossible not to feel a pang of regret – not that he failed to 'fulfil his promise' (as so many have said) but that no-one managed to write a truly significant role for the man. An actor can only do so much, and a large part of Brando's achievement is that he manages to make Kazan's and Bertolucci's films look as if they mean something while we are watching them. Norman Mailer called *Last Tango* 'a failure worth a hundred films like *The Godfather*', and as far as Brando's performance was concerned, he was right. But Hollywood rewards its own and it was for his portrayal of Don Vito Corleone that Brando was awarded his second Oscar.

In 1971 George C. Scott had upset the Motion Picture Academy by refusing to accept the Oscar for Best Actor that he was awarded for his portrayal of *Patton*. The astonished outrage that greeted this 'snub' failed to acknowledge Scott's consistency. Ten years before, he had declined the Best Supporting Actor nomination for his role as Bert Gordon in *The Hustler* – as he had not won on that occasion, few people made any fuss. Scott's distaste for the empty competitiveness of the Oscar ceremony was shared by many of his colleagues but they recognised that, in Peter Ustinov's words: '..to refuse awards…is another way of accepting them with more noise than is usual.' Scott has since gone on record as saying that his attempt to distance himself from the self-congratulatory world of award shows achieved nothing but the defeat of his purpose.

Brando went one better than Scott when it came to the award for *The Godfather*. Whereas Scott had ignored the award and the ceremony, Brando sent a representative – a young American Indian calling herself Sasheen Littlefeather – to refuse the award on his behalf and make a four-page 'non-acceptance' speech attacking Hollywood for its stereotypical portrayal of the Native American. Predictably, Miss Littlefeather was unable to read the whole speech in the alotted two minutes and was encouraged to leave the stage which she did as graciously as possible, given that she was being vigorously booed at the time.

Brando found little sympathy for his behaviour to the Academy, even from the liberal members of the Hollywood community. Gregory Peck – whose anti-Vietnam stance led to his producing *The Trial of the Catonsville Nine* – suggested that Brando would have been better

Sasheen Littlefeather explaining to puzzled presenters Roger Moore and Liv Ullmann that Brando cannot accept his 1973 Oscar for The Godfather *because of Hollywood's negative treatment of the American Indian.*

Brando addresses a celebrity gathering at the Waldorf Hotel, New York, in 1973. He hosted the event to raise money for the American Indian Movement (AIM).

advised giving some of his enormous income to the Indians rather than taking the rather cowardly course of humiliating Miss Littlefeather. John Wayne, Brando's political opposite, found the episode 'sad' and said: 'If he had something to say, he should have appeared that night and stated his views instead of taking some little unknown girl and dressing her up in an Indian outfit.'

That Brando's gesture had backfired was clear even before the end of the ceremony, with presenters like Clint Eastwood, Rock Hudson and Raquel Welch making feeble quips at Brando's expense to the obvious approval of the audience. Soon afterwards, there was general delight at the revelation in Rona Barrett's gossip column that Miss Littlefeather was actually a small-time actress called Maria Cruz who had won the title of Miss American Vampire of 1970. Worse than that was the judgement of Chief Dan George, himself a Squamish Indian and Oscar recipient, who described Hollywood's current treatment of his people as 'accurate and decent', saying that Brando's little speech came 'ten years too late'.

Those like Peck who wanted Brando to share his income with the Indians may not have realised that he was fast becoming the financial bulwark of AIM (the American Indian Movement). In 1973 he bought forty acres of Californian land which had once belonged to the Chumash tribe and returned it to the Indians with apologies for 'being two hundred years too late'. His dedication to the Indian cause extended to support for AIM's activists and help with legal costs to defend them against harassment and prosecution. One AIM member said: 'Brando was always there when AIM wanted him. He made himself totally available. Much of what he did has not been recorded and he has never received the thanks he deserved. There were those in the movement who kept taking and taking from Brando, and he would always give. He never said no to any request and, as a result, some elements came close to bleeding him dry. But he was an immense inspiration to many of us and I am not alone in feeling an enormous debt of gratitude to Brando for his work on AIM's behalf.'

As far as the Oscar protest is concerned, Sasheen Littlefeather was certainly a member of the Native American Affirmative Image Committee (whatever her real name was) and Brando was absent because he was travelling to Wounded Knee, South Dakota to join a demonstration by the Oglala Sioux. Over the next few years Brando would attempt to re-iterate his protest in a way that Hollywood might find acceptable – with a movie. To illustrate one of the key phrases of his controversial speech ('if we are not our brother's keeper, at least let us not be his executioner') he considered making a film of Dee Brown's highly-acclaimed book of Indian history, *Bury My Heart at Wounded Knee*. The film eventually came to nothing but not before Brando had discussed the project with Martin Scorsese (who was beginning to establish his reputation) and Gillo Pontecorvo (whom Brando had forgiven for the problems on *Queimada!*). With the best will in the world, it is immensely difficult to make an intelligent film on an unpopular subject in Hollywood – and Brando was not accorded the best will in the world.

Brando continued to donate large sums to AIM and other Native American organisations, but he also had to support his extensive family: with three marriages behind him and homes in California and the South Pacific, the cost of this was prohibitive. He had been a film star for thirty years, but he wanted to be something more substantial. Hollywood columnists mocked him for his adherence to causes; even those he helped mocked him. On one occasion, Brando arrived in Wisconsin to mediate with a militant organisation calling itself the Menimonee Warrior Society, which was holding a white family hostage in an attempt to seize land. As the police prepared for a seige, Brando and other members of AIM camped in the vicinity spending days in negotiation with both sides and, eventually, achieving some kind of resolution. But Brando's presence was not universally welcomed by the Menimonee and – in a grotesque parody of a scene from *The Godfather* – a group of them placed a decapitated horse's head in his sleeping bag, reducing the actor to tears.

Brando's position in relation to Native Americans and American blacks is akin to that of a Righteous Gentile during the Nazi Holocaust.

His commitment cost him dear and, if he has never spoken out against the ingratitude he often faced, his frustration has surfaced again and again in interviews. When Connie Chung asked Brando why he had not made a film to depict the true history of the Native American, Brando stared at her coldly and said; 'You are making me really angry now...because I want to tell you in simple chapter and verse that I have tried to get on before the American public, before the world, a movie about the American Indians and the manner in which we committed, as a country, genocide against those people...and I have been told to take a flying you-know-what in a rolling donut.' Claiming to have spent ten years writing scripts and submitting them to film studios and television networks, Brando concluded: 'They don't want to hear about it, they don't want to hear that America followed a policy of genocide.'

That was Brando speaking in 1989, fifteen years after his film of *Bury My Heart at Wounded Knee* had been announced with a cast list that included Steve McQueen, Paul Newman, Jane Fonda and Barbra Streisand. But big stars bring with them big egos and commercial pressures that usually result in craven artistic compromise, so it is not surprising that the film was never made. Brando's frustration can only have been increased by the film he did make after *Last Tango*, an uneven western which he hoped would be 'a serious study of the American Indian'. *The Missouri Breaks* proved to be a serious study of nothing but the inflated reputations of its two stars, Brando and Jack Nicholson.

Brando had been brought into this project by Elliott Kastner, the producer of *The Night of the Following Day* and *The Nightcomers* (warning enough one would have thought, even if the new film did not have 'night' in the title). The director of *The Missouri Breaks* was Arthur Penn, who had worked well with Brando on *The Chase*, and the screenwriter was Thomas McGuane. The script called for Brando to play a character called Robert E. Lee Clayton, a hired gunman tracking down rustlers, led by Nicholson – it had nothing to do with Indians, being in every sense of the word a cowboy story. There were many anomalies: Brando played his role with a thick Irish accent, but why would an Irishman be named after the Confederate general? In fact, why would anyone of middle age be named 'Robert E. Lee' in the 1880s, only twenty years after Lee came to real prominence?

After seeing *The Missouri Breaks*, the Irish actor Richard Harris – who managed to remain friends with Brando after the difficulties of *Mutiny on the Bounty* – sent a telegram to his former co-star. 'Dear Marlon,' he wrote, 'It's very flattering to me because whereas the entire younger generation are spending all their time imitating you, it's grand to find you imitating me.' Brando enjoyed Harris's joke, and returned the compliment by praising Harris for his role in *A Man Called Horse* which portrayed American Indians in a sympathetic light.

As for *The Missouri Breaks*, Brando was disappointed with the final script and hammed up his role at every opportunity. He got along well with Jack Nicholson – they had just become neighbours in Beverly Hills – but, as Andrew Sarris wrote in the *Village Voice*: 'You really have to see Brando and Nicholson to experience the extraordinary lack of electricity between them.' Brando's weight had risen to an ungainly 250 pounds and, according to Thomas McGuane, he had to have his lines written on his horse's neck.

He was well-paid for the role. 'We took the money and ran,' Penn later remarked, '...that was the movie that broke the million-dollar barrier for two actors – Brando and Nicholson got one and a quarter million each for that film.' The cynicism behind the film was not lost on the critics. In the *New Republic*, Stanley Kauffman reported that Brando was 'making a complete ass of himself...If Brando doesn't like acting, why doesn't he quit?'

Kauffman was missing the point. Brando had won himself another Oscar, he had re-established his reputation as a major actor and as a Hollywood rebel, he had just taken one and a quarter million dollars for five and a half weeks work – he was bankable again and he would use that bankability to do even less work for even more money. Success was indeed the best revenge.

Brando as Robert E Lee Clayton in The Missouri Breaks.

11

The end of the affair

WHEN THE news broke that Brando was to be reunited with Francis Ford Coppola for a film version of Joseph Conrad's *Heart of Darkness*, transposing the action from Africa to Vietnam, hopes were raised that the actor would again be on his mettle.

Heart of Darkness, with its central theme of the conflict of civilisations and its tale of one man's quest to find another who has 'gone native' and, in the process, transformed himself into a local god, was a story long-cherished by Orson Welles. Welles had been planning a film of Conrad's novella since the beginning of his career, but it never happened. Coppola, on the other hand, saw in the story strong links with the American experience in Vietnam – which had become a very real 'heart of darkness' for a generation of young Americans. The Coppola version would be renamed *Apocalypse Now* and made by his own company, Zoetrope, with backing from United Artists and a variety of other world-wide distributors. The film's budget was estimated in excess of $20 million and United Artists sought to protect their investment by demanding that Coppola fill at least one of the two main roles with a star name. These roles were Willard, the questor, and Kurtz – a smaller but no less significant role – the object of the quest.

Coppola, who had originally planned to produce the film with George Lucas as director, took over the direction in the wake of *The Godfather*'s success. He first tried to satisfy United Artists by casting Steve McQueen as Willard, but McQueen declined because he did not want to spend a long period on location. Coppola then turned to the proven combination of Brando and Al Pacino, but Pacino was too busy to play Willard and Brando showed no interest in Kurtz. McQueen was then offered Kurtz with James Caan as Willard, but Caan wanted

Brando as Colonel Kurtz in Apocalypse Now. *After* The Godfather *and* Last Tango in Paris, *Brando was again being used as a cinematic icon.*

$2 million and McQueen $3 million – a budgetary combination for which Coppola felt he could get a much bigger name than Caan's. He approached Jack Nicholson, who proved too busy to play Willard or – when Coppola later renewed his offer – Kurtz. Finally after Coppola had tried to set up deals with Robert Redford, Nicholson and McQueen, Brando changed his mind and offered to play Kurtz for $3.5 million plus a percentage of the film's profits.

With Brando as Kurtz, United Artists were content to let Coppola dispense with a star name for Willard. He chose Harvey Keitel – who had distinguished himself in his work for Martin Scorsese. Location shooting began in the Philippines but ground to a halt when Coppola and Keitel clashed over the actor's interpretation of his role. Keitel was fired and, following a chance encounter with Coppola at Los Angeles airport, Martin Sheen was brought in to replace him. Sheen, a dedicated and ambitious performer, arrived on location and threw himself into the role with such fervour that he suffered a heart attack. At this stage there was no question of re-casting and Sheen's recovery period added to the film's mounting cost. The production was further delayed by savage weather conditions and earthquakes. With principal photography not even properly under way, *Apocalypse Now* was being dubbed 'Coppola's Folly' by many film industry insiders.

Once again, Coppola was using Brando's cinematic reputation to the film's advantage. Colonel Kurtz is not seen until the end of the film, when he is on screen for little more than ten minutes, but his presence must dominate the action, lending an air of real anticipation to the climax when Willard – appointed by the Army to find and kill Kurtz – finally tracks him down. During his journey, Willard encounters a gallery of memorable characters, chief among them being Robert Duvall as the aptly-named Lt. Colonel Kilgore who leads his helicopter squad on a raid to the strains of 'The Ride of the Valkyries', and Dennis Hopper as a drug-crazed photo-journalist whose character was reputedly based on the British war photographer, Tim Page.

Leaving aside John Wayne's misbegotten apologia for the war in *The Green Berets*, the Vietnam experience had hitherto been shunned by mainstream film-makers and Coppola was among the first to tackle the subject head-on. What made the film acceptable to many was Coppola's attempt to transform America's shabby, interventionist action into something approaching a modern myth rooted in the artistic soil of Conrad's original story. Many scenes that seemed excessive were found to have been based on fact: there really were commanders who led combat missions to musical accompaniment – although it was more often as not the Rolling Stones rather than Wagner – and Tim Page's wild behaviour is well documented in Michael Herr's Vietnam memoir, *Despatches* and the photographer's own autobiography, *Page by Page*.

That the film dealt primarily with the American experience of the

war is perhaps inevitable, but it also set the tone for future treatments of the theme – epic stories overladen with classical or rock music – from Michael Cimino's woefully dishonest *The Deer Hunter* to Oliver Stone's *Platoon*.

After the visual pyrotechnics that pepper the earlier parts of the film, Brando's appearance in *Apocalypse Now* threatens to come as something of an anti-climax. Indeed, it is hard at first to conceive of the threat that this rambling, poetry-quoting madman with his obsessive air is supposed to pose to the Army establishment. But the film has been slowly building toward the confrontation between Willard and Kurtz. As the moment approaches, Coppola's casting of Brando seems more and more appropriate. Willard listens to tape-recordings of Kurtz's voice, reads reports of his military record and studies photographs of him with the eyes of an admiring colleague. He seems to be identifying with him, and it is not too fanciful to draw parallels with the way that actors of Sheen's generation identified with

The quarry and the hunter. Kurtz (Brando) is tracked down by Willard (Martin Sheen) in Apocalypse Now.

Brando.

When they finally meet, Willard approaches his quarry with awe. Kurtz is revealed as part mystic, part madman – a warrior-poet. He quotes from Eliot's 'The Hollow Men' – which takes its epigraph from Conrad's story – and relates a grim tale of his experiences with an American unit which had innoculated the children of an enemy village against disease. Kurtz admits that he wept when he re-entered the village to find that the childrens' innoculated arms had been chopped off by their own soldiers. Then, he says, he began to appreciate the genius of an enemy which had learned to cut itself off from human sensitivity in the interests of winning a war. Americans could not do this, which is why they could never win in Vietnam. The implication is that Kurtz, as an American, is basically sensitive and – despite his new-found savagery – is therefore in pain. He almost welcomes Willard – his assassin – and Willard begins to view his appointed task as merciful. The film is not concerned with the wider implications of the American presence in the region, its underlying theme is one of a modern American tragedy – the desensitising of an honourable American Officer.

Only when Kurtz dies, with Conrad's famous words: 'The horror, the horror...' on his lips, do we realise the full weight of Coppola's enormous conceit. White America, having all but obliterated its own continent's native peoples and their culture, craves new myths and legends. Coppola provides one by using the iconography of literature (Conrad, Eliot, and, *en passant*, *The Golden Bough*), and cinema (Brando) to lend a pseudo-artistic patina to what is finally nothing more than a big-budget war movie with a college education. How appropriate that George Lucas should have been put forward as the film's original director. Lucas was the director of the *Star Wars* trilogy, the expensive fantasy whose comic-book simplicity was embraced by the respected myth-gatherer, Joseph Campbell. Willard and Kurtz are the dark sides of Luke Skywalker and Darth Vader – unable to deal with reality.

There would be echoes of *Apocalypse Now* in Brando's next, unrealised project whose themes owed much to Joseph Conrad and which he originated with the help of the British film director, Donald Cammell. Cammell's reputation rests on the cult success of the 1968 thriller *Performance* which he co-directed with Nicolas Roeg. Since then he has made only two other features, *Demon Seed* (1977) and *White of the Eye* (1988), neither of which did anything to soften his position as a cinematic outsider. Cammell was a Paris-based painter when he was first introduced to Brando by Christian Marquand during the filming of *The Young Lions*. They did not stay in touch but Brando remembered Cammell when he saw, and was impressed by *Performance* – which had a delayed release in the United States.

Just as he had invited Stanley Kubrick to direct *One-Eyed Jacks* and Martin Scorsese to take on the Wounded Knee project, so Brando asked Cammell if he would be interested in directing *Fan Tan*, a Conradian tale of an adventurer's journey into the South China Seas.

At the time Cammell was already working on *Demon Seed*, a straightforward science fiction story which is best remembered for a scene in which Julie Christie is 'raped' by a computer. Having taken over that film from the original director, Brian de Palma, Cammell welcomed the opportunity to work on the creation of a screenplay – which Brando proposed they should write together – and to direct Brando in his first major role since *Last Tango*. Looking back on the experience, Cammell told the British documentarist Chris Rodley: 'I've talked with Bertolucci about it and he worked with Marlon much the way I do. Which is with a lot of *affection*. I think it just becomes tedious to go into all the intimacies of the kind of relationship you have with someone who's going to become part of an imaginary world on the screen. But my attitude is that one does anything that's necessary. You humiliate yourself all the time, within the confines of that experience.'

Just how much humiliation Cammell had to endure became clear when, after three months' work on Tetiaroa and the completion of a 150-page treatment, Brando suddenly decided to scrap the whole project. Despite interest from a major studio, Brando could not be persuaded to carry on. 'Marlon changed his mind about it for reasons related to his general problems in executing material he's created himself.' Cammell explained. 'The excuses he used were the expense of the picture, the fact that it had to be a studio movie, that he wanted to produce it independently, to keep control. That nothing could be done through the Hollywood majors. It was one of those burdens he invents for himself...it's idealism. To be in his own movie, one he feels he's created as a writer, is something he truly wants and desires and needs. He's so ambitious and idealistic. But being an idealist and a perfectionist can become very destructive...a crazy, self-defeating limitation.'

Brando then suggested that Cammell write a novel based on the film treatment – with the sale of the novel providing the necessary capital to finance the film independently. Cammell dutifully set to work on a novel which, he claimed, 'encapsulated a picture of Marlon himself. A fundamentally dishonest man. A man who made his living dishonestly and made enough to get himself a schooner of his own and go south in his middle years to find pearls.' This crypto-Brando was named, at the actor's insistence, Annie Dowltry. Cammell was half-way through the book and had collected substantial advances when Brando once again called a halt.

The final budget of *Apocalypse Now* reached $31.5 million, and the film did not open until 1979 – three years after production started – and by that time Brando had completed work on another film, again in a cameo role. This time he took a logical step nearer the world of *Star Wars* in the film version of an earlier manifestation of the modern American mythical hero, *Superman*.

Jay Kanter had long since become totally absorbed in film production, and Brando was now represented by his lawyer, Norman Garey who had negotiated his fee on *Apocalypse Now* and would make an even better deal on his client's behalf for *Superman*. Here, Brando was cast as the hero's father, Jor-El, who despatches his son to an unknown destination rather than allow him to die in the destruction of his home planet, Krypton. Brando was required for only twelve days of shooting and Garey arranged for him to receive $3.7 million for his time on the film. The director was Richard Donner, who had recently enjoyed a success with the first of the *Omen* series of horror films. Donner was well aware of the responsibility of directing a big-budget film, but now he had to bear in mind the expense of a big-budget star. 'Knowing how little time we had with Brando,' he recalled, 'I'd even been figuring out what it would cost us every time he went to the lavatory.'

Along with his old sparring partner, Trevor Howard, Brando was featured in the film's opening twenty minutes solely as a device to lend 'star power' to a film whose leading role was played by the then unknown Christopher Reeve. His performance as Jor-El is unremarkable and could have been given by any actor of competence.

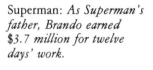

Superman: *As Superman's father, Brando earned $3.7 million for twelve days' work.*

Brando, the antithesis of Hollywood commercialism in the fifties, had become its greatest exponent in the seventies.

Brando's declared distaste for acting seemed to go hand-in-hand with his development as a cameo performer. For a few million dollars, 'the world's greatest film actor' would turn up on a movie set for a few days and give an undistinguished film the necessary box office cachet. Remarking on this lucrative tendency, Billy Wilder observed: 'Mr. Marlon Brando got, for an aggregate of twenty minutes on screen in *Superman* and *Apocalypse Now*, more money than Clark Gable got for twenty years at MGM.' Nor was this absurdity confined to the big screen. In 1979, just before he travelled to England to make *Superman*, Brando made a brief apearance in the television series, *Roots: the Next Generations*.

Based on Alex Haley's best-selling novel which charted the Black experience in North America, the original series of *Roots* had been an enormous success for the ABC television company. It was not surprising then that the network sought to make a sequel that brought the history of Haley's characters and their descendants up to date. The complete story finished, in classic Hollywood style, by depicting Haley himself – played by James Earl Jones – finding the need to document the history of the American Black and so beginning work on his original novel. One of Haley's most extraordinary assignments as a journalist had been his interview with the notorious racist leader of the American Nazi Party, George Lincoln Rockwell, for *Playboy* magazine. Rockwell would become the least mourned of the political figures who fell to assassins' bullets in the 'sixties.

Brando had admired the first series of *Roots* and he approached Haley to offer his services when he heard of the planned sequel. Insisting on playing a villain he suggested that he would be content with a small role and his casting as Rockwell seemed to satisfy both criteria. In the event, Brando's performance gained him an Emmy – television's Oscar – as Best Supporting Actor and, *pace* Billy Wilder, he donated his undisclosed fee to charity.

While Brando was very good as Rockwell, he was not really an ideal choice. He lent the man a degree of glamour which he had neither possessed nor deserved. It would have suited the series better if the part had been cast with a less 'high profile' actor – and also someone who was not so timid about showing the true villainy of the man. Brando lends all his villains a considerable charm – which can be very effective at times – but he never lets us feel the meanness of spirit that lurks beneath it. A villain's charm should be sardonic – one thinks of James Mason or Claude Rains – and the actor playing him should be unafraid of exploring the dark side of the character. As Rockwell, Brando was playing a man whose professed beliefs were totally at odds with his own but the actor can be glimpsed, peering from behind the mask and

Brando and James Earl Jones recreate journalist Alex Haley's interview with American Nazi Lincoln Rockwell for the television series Roots: The Next Generations. *Brando's performance won him an Emmy but he was an unconvincing villain.*

flashing his liberal credentials. Mindful of the confusion between actor and role that had dogged his career, Brando may have found it difficult to lay himself open to the outright contempt that Rockwell's bigotry would provoke, but he could at least have hinted at the sense of danger within his character. He settles instead for a 'star turn'.

He was a lamentably unsuccessful villain again in his next role – another cameo – in John G. Avildsen's 1980 thriller, *The Formula*. The real interest here was that Brando was cast against George C. Scott – a considerable actor who has suffered almost as much as Brando from being cast in inferior material.

The Formula was well-named, in that it was a formulaic entertainment of a kind that was very nearly played out many years before: a modern conspiracy story featuring the legacy of the Third Reich and the misdeeds of big business. In this case, Scott played Barney Caine, a detective trying to solve a friend's murder and coming across evidence that the dead man had knowledge of a secret energy-saving formula developed by the Nazis but suppressed by the international oil industry. Caine's investigations lead him to the oil tycoon, Adam Steiffel (Brando) whose machinations seem to be at the root of things.

Both Scott and Brando are on record as saying that they considered the film to have something important to say about the way that businessmen – in particular those involved in such powerful organisations as oil cartels - manipulate society against its best interests. The team of Avildsen and Steve Shagan, who wrote the original novel and screenplay, had only recently won acclaim for the film *Save the Tiger* in which Jack Lemmon gave an Oscar-winning performance as a businessman on the verge of a nervous breakdown, the anti-corporate attitude of *The Formula* was what attracted Brando to the film, and Shagan was clearly a writer of intelligence.

Adam Steiffel is seen in only three brief scenes – two quite early in the film and one very near the end – but, as Caine's search for the truth brings him back to the tycoon, Steiffel assumes a malevolent importance in the story. Scott gives an intelligent performance, coping well with Caine's platitudinous philosophising in the concluding scenes. The theatre critic Walter Kerr has written well about Scott's style of acting – 'thinking matters through freshly scene by scene' – and it has always struck me that it is an actor like Scott, and not Brando, that younger actors should really watch and learn to emulate. But Scott himself is one of Brando's many professional admirers and one who uses the word 'genius' to describe him. After working with Brando, Scott remarked: 'I'm not the least surprised that he doesn't want to work or that he wants eighty zillion dollars to work. I mean, if I were him, I would have told them to go fuck themselves a long time ago.'

Despite his solidarity with a fellow performer, Scott is as ill-served in his scenes with Brando as many other good actors have been. Brando's Adam Steiffel is a fussy, lazy performance with not trace of the dynamism that had last been evident in Bertolucci's film. Portly, and with a bald head across which are scraped a few strands of hair, Brando sports a dental plate that would be the envy of Jerry Lewis in *The Nutty Professor*. His portrayal is unconvincing as a portrait of a man of power and, even if it can be argued that the character's insouciance is evidence of his certainty about his position, it is marked by an extraordinary lack of concern about the drama of a scene. In the final confrontation between Caine and Steiffel, Scott is forceful and direct but he is faced with a man who proffers candy ('milk duds') and potters about his office adjusting a clock, fiddling with his suit, looking out of windows – in short, sabotaging the film's

Brando as Adam Steiffel with George C. Scott in The Formula.

denouement. When Caine leaves the office, confident that he has at least struck a small blow against Steiffel by passing the formula on to the Swiss, Steiffel picks up the telephone and arranges for the Swiss themselves to further suppress the secret, thus restoring the status quo. Brando's air of deliberate calm robs this final twist of any real value – we already know that Scott's ploy has been ineffective. The director's desperation shows when Scott takes his leave of Brando with the words: 'If I didn't have a son I'd splatter your brains all over this room.' At this point there are two fast cuts from Scott's face in close-up to Brando's. The cuts look odd, but are clearly there to add the missing dramatic quality. Avildsen, or his editor, is being clumsy – but who

169

can blame him? Brando has drained the scene of all impact.

Steve Shagan was speaking of both Scott and Brando when he said: 'I sensed a loss of purpose, a sense of betrayal, a feeling that they don't want to work anymore, a sense that they have come to think of acting as playing with choo-choo trains.' Scott would soon follow Brando's lead into the realms of absurdity, playing Mussolini in a television mini-series and repeating his acclaimed portrayal of General Patton for an indifferent sequel (again for television). Like Brando, he remains an actor whose considerable talent is not best-suited to the confines of stardom.

The Formula was not a success and Brando's diminishing public was, in any case, not interested in seeing its idol looking short, fat and bald – even though that happened to be the way he was at the age of fifty-six. The sight of Marlon Brando like this made his contemporaries feel old, and it was harder still to convince the new generation of filmgoers that he had ever been anything special. Brando the actor no longer excited audience expectations and in any case he publicly scorned his talent and mocked those who still admired him. He still affected to spurn Hollywood, but he remained essentially a Hollywood star. But now his earnestness was beginning to bore people and, even those who sympathised with him found it hard to believe that an actor of his standing could not get a worthwhile project off the ground. He was no longer seen as a rebel, but as just another rich, fat actor who spouted liberal phrases and belittled the only thing that set him apart, that fed his success. It was an appropriate moment for him to leave his admirers with their memories and simply retire. For a time, it seemed that he had done just that, and that the love affair between Hollywood and its favourite rebel was finally over.

If Brando's disaffection with film acting appeared to have reached its inevitable conclusion, his private life still gave rise to speculation. The press began to treat him as a 'fallen idol', in the classic tradition of American artists who failed to fulfill the promise of their early careers. Many commentators saw a likeness to Elvis Presley – a one-time sex symbol who had become an overweight recluse. Presley's life, and his death at the early age of 42, was already being written up as an American tragedy: the price of fame or a warning against the 'deification' conferred upon him. The question is whether the warning should be intended for the likes of Presley or for his fans. Like Presley, Brando has an appeal which is based as much on his audience's sexual fantasy as on his own talent. Should he be blamed for the power that others have invested in him?

The tales that abounded in the seventies and eighties were of a man who was increasingly isolated – by choice and circumstance. Several of Brando's friends died during this period. Wally Cox, whose television fame had been shortlived, suffered a prolonged crisis of confidence which contributed to the heart disease which killed him in 1972 at the early age of 48. Brando, deeply distressed by Cox's death, was forced to hide from waiting journalists while paying his respects to the bereaved family. William Redfield – who had written so sharply about Brando in 'Letters From an Actor' – also died, as did two other veterans of the ill-fated 'Arms and the Man' tour: Sam Gilman, who had remained a close friend, and Carlo Fiore. Fiore had had problems with drug addiction throughout his life, and Brando had funded a number of de-toxification programs for him. On Brando's recommendation, Fiore was hired as his stand-in for *On the Waterfront*, and thereafter often worked in one capacity or another on Brando's films. When Brando finally fell out of touch with him, Fiore published, in 1974, a pathetically self-important memoir of their friendship.

Other, violent deaths also touched Brando. Anne Ford, a fashion designer who had been his companion during the filming of *Waterfront* was murdered by thieves in her apartment; a more recent girlfriend, the actress Jill Banner was killed in a car accident.

However well the middle-aged Brando might have prepared himself for the intimations of mortality contained in the deaths of these friends and lovers, he was profoundly shocked by the suicide of his agent, Norman Garey in August 1982. The lucrative payments he had arranged for Brando's services had gained Garey an enviable reputation as a deal-maker. His client list expanded to include Francis Ford Coppola and Gene Hackman, as well as musicians like Quincy Jones and Elton John. He was still a relatively young man – over ten years younger than Brando – and his future seemed assured. His suicide – brought about by the side-effects of prescribed drug use – sent a shockwave of disbelief throughout the Hollywood community.

But even Garey's death could not outweigh the issue that most dominated Brando's private life: the legacy of his unfortunate marriage to Anna Kashfi. Like Fiore, Kashfi had written a book about Brando in the wake of his success with *The Godfather* and *Last Tango*. There had been an eager readership for the kind of salacious memoir that Fiore had turned out in *Bud – the Brando I knew* which had been touted as 'his best friend's story'. In 1979, Kashfi published 'the wife's story', *Brando for Breakfast*', which detailed her version of their short marriage and the ensuing custody battle over their son, Christian.

The question of custody had arisen almost immediately after the failure of the marriage in September 1959 with Brando and Kashfi simultaneously alleging the other's unsuitablity for parenthood. Kashfi took Brando to court, portraying him as a wife-beater, while he countered with a claim against her for breaking into his house. Christian – or Devi, as Kashfi insisted on calling him – spent the next few years as a human shuttlecock until, in 1964, Brando won custody of him. The overwhelming factor against Kashfi at the time

Anna Kashfi lashes out (right) at Brando (in pigtail) as they leave a Santa Monica courtroom in 1961 during one of their early custody battles over their son, Christian. The custody battles, chronicled with vitriol in Kashfi's autobiography (below), continued until 1971 when Brando and Kashfi were awarded joint custody.

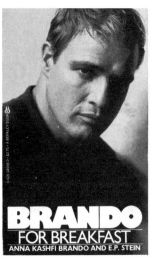

was her acknowledged addiction to drugs and alcohol, but she was to win her son back less than a year later when she convinced an appeal court that her problems were under control. Now it was Brando who seemed comparatively unstable. Still married to Movita, he was living on Tetiaroa with Tarita Teriipia by whom he had had another son, Tehitou, in 1963. In 1971 – by which time Brando's marriage to Movita was annulled and he had had a second child, a daughter called Cheyenne, by Tarita – he and Kashfi were awarded joint custody of Christian with a court stipulation that the boy should become a boarder at a Californian school.

This uneasy compromise was reached just before Brando's return to public favour with *The Godfather*. As his fortunes rose, so Kashfi went into decline. Her alcohol problems returned and were highlighted when in 1972 she effectively had Christian kidnapped from his school and taken to Mexico where he was quickly traced and Kashfi was arrested. Brando's re-established career, in contrast to Kashfi's clearly disturbed behaviour, led him to be granted sole custody and Kashfi was pushed to the margin of Christian's life. Norman Garey's contractual dealings on Brando's behalf appeared to ensure a high level of financial security for the actor's dependants and the drama that had attended the first fourteen years of Christian's life was assumed to be at an end.

As Brando's film appearances became less frequent, finally being

Brando with his 13-year-old son Christian attending yet another custody hearing in Santa Monica (left). In fact, after Anna Kashfi had Christian effectively kidnapped from his school and taken to Mexico in 1972, Brando was awarded sole custody of his son. Brando's daughter Cheyenne (below) by his third wife Tarita, on the island of Tetiaroa where she was brought up.

restricted to the increasingly lack-lustre cameos, there was speculation that he was planning a return to leading roles with a personal project, such as the much-discussed Wounded Knee film. But his devotion to minority politics and environmental issues proved an immense drain on his time as well as his income. After *The Formula* he was absent from the screen for nine years. In his 1989 television interview with Connie Chung, Brando gave an unsatisfactory account of his long period of inactivity, claiming to find acting 'odious, unpleasant', and stressing his interest in writing.

If Brando himself was not forthcoming, the British film director Donald Cammell had more to say about the use Brando had been making of his time. Brando and Cammell did not meet again until after the filming of *White of the Eye*, Cammell's 1988 feature which centred on the story of a serial killer and ran into trouble with the American censors. Brando saw the film in a private screening and was so enthusiastic about it that he wrote a letter to the censors praising it as a work of 'originality, artistry and power, blessedly devoid of intellectual posturing' and urging them not to withhold the necessary 'R' certificate that would ensure the film's distribution beyond the hard-core sex and violence circuit. He also telephoned Cammell and invited him to direct a film that Brando would star in and write – alone this time – *Jericho*.

173

Jericho took its title from the code-name of CIA veteran, Billy Harrington (Brando) who is lured from retirement to undertake a last mission – the assassination of a Colombian drug baron. When he refuses, the CIA engineer a meeting between his daughter and the Colombian's son, who falls in love with her. 'The CIA are double-crossing both sides,' Cammell told Chris Rodley, 'They kidnap the daughter to lure Jericho down there so that they can blackmail the Colombian drug lord into handing over extra money to support Central American insurgence by saying Jericho is coming to assassinate the boy's father. In fact, he's being fed to the lions because he's really only on a mission to save his daughter...He kidnaps the drug baron's son and executes him in front of them, thereby ensuring war between the Colombians and the CIA. Then he kills...well, he kills everybody. Everybody! In the last reel.

'A lot of the more interesting moments are meditations and soliloquies from Jericho, in the bunker below his house in Mexico, as he looks back on his life. He's a man at the end of the road. The overall image of the film is of a man living with his own guilt over all the horror he's perpetrated. But he's given absolution. He's pardoned, and his daughter is returned to him.'

This excessively violent tale was to have been produced by Elliot Kastner – who should have known better by now – for Trans World Entertainment, and expectations ran high. There was no problem in raising money for the film, according to Cammell: 'There were many sources of finance immediately open – a *choice* of finance.' Furthermore, the experience on *Fan Tan* had prepared Cammell for the delays that might be caused by Brando's slow working methods. The problem lay with the script which Brando insisted on writing alone. 'Writing a piece of drama is not the same as improvising within a story already given to you by Bertolucci or Coppola,' Cammell observed. 'Marlon loves to think that he wants to create other characters, but in fact his main interest is always his own. His other characters tend to be sketchy...when you get material from Marlon that oscillates from brilliant, imaginative, juicy, inspired characterisation, to vacuums where the process has become a child-like copying of some TV show, you're really faced with a difficult job.'

With Brando unable to complete a workable script, Cammell's problems were increased by the production company's obsession with Brando's immense bulk, brought about by years of over-eating. 'I thought his weight was perfect for the role,' said Cammell, 'I thought of him as a sumo wrestler...But the producers were still thinking of him as the young Brando. They kept talking about him as Mark Antony, which he played in 1953.'

The last blow came when Brando – despite having long scheduled *Jericho* as his return to the screen – travelled to England in 1988 to

By the late eighties Brando had become a virtual recluse and his weight problem was causing concern for his health.

make a cameo appearance in *A Dry White Season* for the young Martinique director, Euzhan Palcy. Brando was not happy with the result of his work on that film, and he was further reported to be distressed at the sight of himself in the rushes. It was a forcible reminder of his distaste for film acting and it compounded the crisis of confidence he was having with the script of *Jericho*. Although the film was now in an advanced state of pre-production, and he had already received his first advance payment, Brando abandoned *Jericho* and Cammell found his second Brando project collapsing around him.

The cancellation of *Jericho*, however frustrating it may have been for Cammell and Kastner, caused no great surprise in the trade press where the project had been announced with little or no fanfare. Any film with Brando's name attached was now approached with caution and any idea that he would return to leading roles was taken with a pinch of salt.

But if the media had lost confidence in Brando, Donald Cammell had not: 'What's frightening is if Marlon came back to me next year, with all the sardonic jeers I may throw back at him down the phone, I would probably go along. Because there's a depth of affection for him that's based on my day-to-day working with him. And respect for his talent, which has *not* diminished. Because it's so brightly burning inside this fucked-up jungle genius.'

12

Looking for Zeus

I F *Jericho* came to nothing and dashed any immediate hope of Brando's return to leading roles, there was compensation of a sort from his cameo appearance in *A Dry White Season*

Based on a novel by the white South African, André Brink, *A Dry White Season* tells the story of a decent, middle-class white man, Ben de Toit (played by Donald Sutherland) who gradually becomes aware of the social injustices of apartheid. Although it showed the experiences of black people under this cruel regime, the film was essentially the story of a white family and was squarely aimed at a white, liberal audience. Nevertheless, Metro-Goldwyn-Mayer chose Euzhan Palcy as the director, thus making her the first black woman to be placed in charge of a Hollywood project. Palcy had gained an international reputation with her first film, *Rue Cases Negres* which had told of a childhood in the Martinique of her birth. Her connection with South Africa was non-existent but it was enough for Hollywood that she was black and therefore bound to respond to the film's theme.

With such a difficult subject – however much it might be watered down for American tastes – MGM felt it important to have a big star in the cast. As Brando's position on human rights was well-known, he seemed a real possibility even if Palcy considered the likelihood of his accepting the role to be very remote. The role in question was that of Ian McKenzie, the lawyer engaged by de Toit after his black gardener has died in police custody. It was very likely to appeal to Brando's well-known concern for social justice, but Euzhan Palcy considered it an impossible piece of 'dream casting' and was duly astonished when Brando agreed. Not only did he agree to play the role, but he insisted on working for the Screen Actors Guild minimum wage, provided that his usual salary was paid to an anti-apartheid organisation – with MGM

Brando in The Freshman *parodying his Don Corleone image seventeen years after* The Godfather.

176

making a further significant contribution. Although that salary was set at $3.3 million, Brando was also on 11.3% of the film's gross. He told Connie Chung: 'With this picture, as are many pictures today, making $100 million, I probably could stand to make $10 million.'

Brando's gesture was an indication of how highly he regarded Palcy's film, but his return to the screen was not to go smoothly. Palcy was unhappy with the screenplay by the British writer, Colin Welland – who had won an Oscar for his script of *Chariots of Fire* – and she began re-working scenes herself. Brando has said that he wrote and directed his own scenes which amounted to twenty minutes of screen time, climaxing in a sharply-observed courtroom confrontation between McKenzie and the South African police witnesses. Wearing a thick white wig and with wire-rimmed spectacles perched on the end of his nose, Brando moves slowly through these scenes bearing his considerable bulk down onto a walking-stick. There is a wit and energy in his dialogue that is lacking in the rest of the film: 'Justice and the

With Donald Sutherland in A Dry White Season *which marked Brando's return to the screen after an eight-year break, and contained his best cameo performance.*

law are distant cousins,' McKenzie tells de Toit, 'and here in South Africa they're not on speaking terms at all.' There is no doubt that these are the strongest scenes in a film which is marred by simplistic writing and dull acting.

Apart from the disagreements between Palcy and Welland, the film was further altered by MGM itself – much to Brando's displeasure. He told Connie Chung: 'I think [MGM] made a money decision...it's not unreasonable to think the South African government could put a boycott on MGM films.' Brando did not specify the changes that were made by the studio but he was clearly disgusted with the way that his and Palcy's contributions were edited. Certainly, the final impression that the film leaves is one of apartheid as being something ugly in South Africa's *past*, and the policeman who is identified as the villain of the piece and who finally kills Ben de Toit is himself assassinated in the last scene of the film. *A Dry White Season* is riddled with compromise and is finally ineffective both as cinema and as propaganda. Brando wrote to the British actor Michael Gambon, who played the judge in the trial scene: 'I've seen our movie, and they fucked it up. It isn't the first time and it won't be the last.'

In fact, for all his generosity with his salary for *A Dry White Season*, Brando was facing financial difficulties on Tetiaroa and was seriously considering selling it. In 1983 it had been hit by a severe hurricane which as good as destroyed the hotel whose construction Brando had financed. With his abandonment of Donald Cammell's *Jericho* there seemed no immediate way of raising money unless he took on another film role – this time very much as a 'commercial enterprise'.

Brando was therefore in a receptive frame of mind when Andrew Bergman sent him the script of his comedy, *The Freshman*. Bergman had been one of the writers on the Mel Brooks western spoof, *Blazing Saddles*, and had gone on to write two popular comedy-thrillers, *Fletch* and *The In-Laws*. Brando had so enjoyed the last of these that he had called Bergman to praise it and to discuss the possibility of working together on a comedy idea he was developing himself. Brando's comedy came to nothing, but Bergman's partner Mike Lobell suggested sending *The Freshman* script to the actor to see if he might be interested in playing the leading role of a Mafia boss. The part had been written with a younger actor in mind – Bergman was thinking of casting Joe Mantegna who had proved very popular in David Mamet's films *House of Games* and *Things Change*. Brando liked the script and invited Bergman and Lobell to visit him for a week on Tetiaroa. 'We talked about comedy.' Bergman recalled, 'We talked about life. We talked about the Indians. We talked about the Jews and the Holocaust. And then, after a week, I guess he felt comfortable with us. He said, ''Here's a couple of things about how I want to play it. And if you guys agree, I'm in.'' '

The freshman of the film's title is Clark Kellog (Matthew Broderick), a first-year film student who arrives in New York City from Vermont and is immediately conned out of his money and his luggage by Victor Ray (Bruno Kirby), a small-time hustler with mob connections. When Clark tracks down Victor he discovers that the money has been spent and his stolen goods have all but vanished. Victor offers to make it up to Clark by getting him high-paid, part-time work with his uncle Carmine Sabatini (Brando), a prominent figure in 'the import business'.

With Brando in the role of Uncle Carmine, Bergman was able to alter his script to incorporate an elaborate in-joke which made great play of the actor's identification with *The Godfather*. When Victor takes Clark to meet his uncle, they find a Brando who exactly resembles his characterisation of Don Vito Corleone, right down to the whispered accent. 'I know what you're thinking,' Victor tells Clark, 'But he's the original. They based the movie on him.' Nobody actually says *which* movie, but the joke is clearly pointed when we see one of Clark's college lecturers leading study sessions on *Godfather II*.

Whereas in 1972 Brando needed extensive padding and make-up to transform himself into the Mafia chief, the Brando we see in *The Freshman* is able to replicate his appearance with minimal artificial help. The script is peppered with small in-jokes which guy Brando himself as much as they parody the role that won him his second Oscar. Apropos of nothing, Carmine tells Clark: 'I'm really worried about this ozone business; I'm really very concerned' and the movie ends with his offer of help with Clark's film career: 'I know some people in Hollywood.' Neither of these lines is at all funny in itself, but audiences laughed precisely because it was Brando saying them.

Without Brando, *The Freshman* would remain a pleasantly forgettable comedy with one or two nice moments but the clever use of his Godfather persona makes it altogether more watchable. The most delightful revelation was seeing Brando finally make a success of playing comedy. No longer struggling to convince as a comic leading man, he was clearly happier to be cast as a character actor. 'Before we started filming,' Mike Lobell said, 'Brando said to us, "You know, when people laugh, their bodies produce endorphins, and I would like to be responsible for producing an endorphin or two." '

The Freshman gave Brando his first leading role in fifteen years. For the new generation of American filmgoers whose cinematic memories stretched no further back than the latest installments of *Star Wars* or *Indiana Jones* Brando was almost an unknown quantity. When *The Freshman* was shown to preview audiences, several younger members wrote such comments as, 'Who's the old guy? – He's great,' on their preview cards.

Throughout the 60-day shooting period, the cast and crew of *The*

Freshman paid tribute to Brando's helpful and friendly demeanour and credited him with contributing to the generally relaxed atmosphere on the film's Canadian location. This atmosphere was to be shattered during the last few days of filming when Brando received news that his 20-year-old daughter Cheyenne had been involved in a serious car accident which would require her to have plastic surgery. Brando flew to Los Angeles to see Cheyenne and only when she was out of danger did he return to Toronto to film a difficult scene which involved him skating on an ice rink. During the rehearsals for this scene, Brando fell several times and injured his neck. Although he was able to complete the small amount of filming that was left, he was forced to wear a neck-brace when off-camera and was clearly in pain.

On the very last day of shooting, in August 1989, Andrew Bergman was full of praise for his star: 'He's been great. There's never been any tension. He's involved in every scene. He's rehearsed his scenes with the other actors. He's always on time. No tantrums. He threw the wrap party for the cast and crew a few days ago, dropped a bundle, bought gifts for everybody. I love this guy.' Meanwhile the object of Bergman's affection was sitting in his trailer giving a surprise interview – at his own request – to a news journalist from the *Toronto Globe and Mail*. His words hardly bear out Bergman's elation: 'It's horrible', Brando says of *The Freshman*. 'It's going to be a flop but after this I'm retiring. I'm so fed up. This picture, except for the Canadian crew, was an extremely unpleasant experience. I wish I hadn't finished with a stinker. Two more shots and I'm done with this madness...you can't imagine how happy I am.'

Brando with Matthew Broderick in The Freshman.

The Brando interview – recorded by Murray Campbell, a journalist whose knowledge of the actor's past work was, by his own admission, limited – was featured on the front page of the Toronto newspaper and featured a photograph of a grim-faced Brando in his neck brace. It was picked up by newspapers across the world and it left Bergman and Lobell feeling puzzled and hurt. In an attempt to understand their star's behaviour, they attributed his ill temper to his concern for Cheyenne Brando's health, but it then emerged that there had been a misunderstanding about overtime payments due to Brando. Tri-Star, the production company, then made an immediate payment of $50,000 and Brando called Lobell and Bergman to apologise for his comments. He also called Matthew Broderick, Bruno Kirby and Penelope Anne Miller – who played his daughter in the film – and followed these apologies with a press release in which he predicted that *The Freshman* would be 'a very successful film'. He recalled his initial disappointment on seeing the first cut of *On the Waterfront*: 'I left the cutting room unable to look my director, Elia Kazan, in the face', and praised the cast, crew and director of *The Freshman*, concluding that he would be prepared to make a sequel if the occasion presented itself.

'There is no substitute for laughter in this frightened and endlessly twisting world,' he wrote. His explanation for his outburst was that he had been 'experiencing some very trying times of a personal nature'. Lobell and Bergman were satisfied, but their troubles with *The Freshman* were not yet over. As for Brando, the 'endlessly twisting world' held a further shock for him.

The Freshman was due for release in the late summer of 1990 and press screenings had begun when word came that Paramount Pictures – producers of the *Godfather* series – were seeking an injunction to prevent the film being shown. Tri-Star executives were initially puzzled by Paramount's move – Paramount had been approached with the script of *The Freshman* and had turned it down, so they were well aware of the content. Furthermore they had supplied footage from *Godfather II* – it was hard to understand their objection. Paramount's expressed view was that Brando was in breach of contract by parodying the character of Don Vito Corleone but it was more likely that they feared that the publicity accorded to *The Freshman* would take away from the scheduled Christmas release of *Godfather III*, Coppola's long-awaited return to the Corleone saga. The two studios then became involved in an absurd wrangle with Paramount attempting to force a six-month delay on *The Freshman*'s release date and Tri-Star responding by putting its promotional operation into slow-motion.

The situation was finally resolved by Tri-Star's disclaimer on the credits of *The Freshman*: 'Paramount Pictures Corporation is the exclusive owner of all motion picture rights in and to *The Godfather, The Godfather, Part II*, and the character of Don Vito Corleone. Any incidental allusion thereto in this motion picture occurs with the permission of Paramount Pictures Corporation.'

The Freshman opened in August 1990 to reviews which confirmed that Brando was back – not with a bang but with a whimsy. In *Newsweek*, David Ansen called Brando's performance 'delicious' and added: 'His presence alone makes Bergman's movie a treat – and the sight of him on ice skates (don't ask why) provides a demented grace note.' In the *New York Times*, Janet Maslin touched on the iconographic casting of Brando when she wrote: 'Mr. Brando serves...not only as an unexpectedly deft comic actor, but also as a magnificent piece of found art.' The *Toronto Globe and Mail*, which had carried Brando's end-of-shooting interview, praised *The Freshman* as 'an amiable, good-natured, fun-loving flick'. But the approval that greeted Brando's newly-revealed comic talents was cold comfort for the actor himself. By the time the film opened, he was deeply embroiled in a private drama which would consign his comeback to the status of a trivial sideshow.

Christian Brando's troubled childhood had not resolved itself in his adult years. A high-school drop-out at eighteen, Christian had drifted into a succession of jobs – including welding and tree-trimming – which failed to satisfy him or provide him with any real security. In 1981, he married a former schoolfriend, Mary McKenna, who was then a make-up artist based in a cosmetic store. Brando supported Christian and Mary in the first years of their marriage, even providing $17,000 for Mary and her sister to gain control of the cosmetics business. Nevertheless, the marriage lasted only four years and Christian became dependant on drugs and alcohol. In 1987 he went to Italy and, in an unsuccessful attempt to follow in his father's footsteps, played a hit-man in a film called *The Issue at Stake*. Christian had had many film offers and there had long been a number of agents who were willing to put him forward for acting or modelling work, but he had always resisted. The film was a failure and was never widely seen but the following year, at the age of 30, Christian became eligible to draw on a trust fund which his father had set up for him. He now had an annual unearned income of $100,000. Something that had been planned to give him a high degree of financial security was available to fund his excesses. Despite his father's frequent interventions, Christian seemed unable to prevent himself from continued decline.

Against this backdrop, on the night of 16th May 1990, the story of Christian Brando took a savage turn. Police and paramedics were called to Marlon Brando's estate at 12900 Mulholland Drive, Beverly Hills, to find Dag Drollet – the 25-year-old lover of Cheyenne Brando – sprawled dead on a couch in the den. Christian Brando immediately confessed to killing Drollet with a .45 handgun, although he accused his victim of having beaten Cheyenne, and claimed that the killing was accidental. However Cheyenne herself, pregnant with Drollet's child, told the Los Angeles police: 'The shooting was not an accident.'

The novelist and screenwriter, Clancy Sigal, reporting on the incident, wrote: 'We are used to lurid murders in Hollywood: William Desmond Taylor; the Fatty Arbuckle case; Thelma Todd; the knifing of hoodlum Johnny Stompanato by Lana Turner's daughter; Sal Mineo slain in his own garage (while I slept through his screams across the street). And most recently, Erik and Lyle Menendez, two sleek Princeton products, accused of using a 12-bore shotgun to blow out the brains of their wealthy showbiz parents...For all its private luxury, Mulholland Drive – a favourite venue of teenage drag-racers who kill themselves fairly regularly by crashing over its steep cliffs – is full of crazy people...One of the Hillside Strangler victims was found in the back of [Brando's] own LA house, and his next-door neighbour was strangled in his bathroom. Roman Polanski's former wife, Sharon Tate, was murdered in Benedict Canyon, a minute away. Charles Manson terrorised rich hill-dwellers, like Brando, who has admitted pulling a gun on intruders "three or four times".' According to Sigal: 'Death in Hollywood is not democratic. You rate a screaming headline and massed TV cameras only if you're either famous or have a good address. Marlon Brando qualifies on both counts.'

Indeed, the shooting was like manna to the news media which wasted no time in running stories about Brando's 'Wild One' son, or inferring that this was a 'Godfather-style execution'. In most cases, Drollet's name was incorrectly spelled in print and more than one paper ran a colour photograph of Christian Brando which dated from 1987. A close-up, the photograph showed a leering Christian, his face decorated in 'warpaint' for a costume party in Rome. He was variously described as a 'failed actor' or a 'misfit' and the impression was of a pathetic character prone to violent rages as a result of parental neglect. It was clear that, when the case came to trial, Marlon Brando would be judged alongside his son – at least, as far as the media were concerned.

The sad fact is that Brando, while he had tried over the years to protect himself from the fawning attentions of life's gate-crashers, had failed in his efforts to keep them away from his son. As Clancy Sigal reported from the Los Angeles Municipal Court: 'Among Christian's visitors and supporters, you will see a fair sample of the human locusts who feed upon famous names. Unless you have a taste for *Hollywood Babylon* or John Waters films, they aren't a pretty sight.' Anna Kashfi arrived at the County Jail, blaming Marlon for the murder, but Christian refused to see her. His mother no longer figured in his life.

At a preliminary hearing, Christian pleaded not guilty to Drollet's murder, and a trial date was set. However this – and several subsequent dates – had to be postponed because in mid-June Cheyenne Brando flew to Tahiti, apparently to avoid being called as a witness. It was expected that she might return to Los Angeles after the birth of her baby, but by then she was involved in lengthy psychiatric treatment. As the affair continued throughout 1990, in the full glare of publicity, Cheyenne's position as a material witness assumed greater importance for the prosecution and attempts were made to extradite her from Tahiti – which was subject to French law. But, when Cheyenne twice attempted suicide and was taken to Paris for further treatment, it was finally accepted that she was – in the words of her attorney – 'a seriously disturbed young woman'. The murder charge was dropped and, in January 1991, Christian Brando pleaded guilty to manslaughter.

From the moment of Christian's arrest, Marlon Brando stood steadfast in his support of his family and, it must be admitted, in defence of his parental abilities. At one point he put up his Mullholland Drive mansion to secure Christian's bail which had been set at $2 million, and he followed this by placing his, as yet unwritten, autobiography on the market for a further $3 million. Assembled journalists at Los Angeles Municipal Court were granted impromptu press conferences from the normally publicity-shy Brando. He was eager, he said, to correct the image of Christian that was being projected by the world's press.

'Like many young people Christian has broken the law by smoking marijuana,' Brando told reporters. 'He also had a drinking problem and is an alcoholic. But I believe him. He has never lied to me.' Declaring that fame 'robs you of your personality', he deplored the way that Christian's trial was being handled and reported like a 'zoo and animal show' just because he was the son of a famous father. 'Let them call me names,' he said, 'It doesn't hurt me. But my children aren't used to that. My son isn't a "mad dog killer" and I hate to see him portrayed in that way...there is another view. There is another Christian. I hope to have the opportunity to present that in court.' When one reporter commended Brando's spiritual strength and asked where he found it, the actor's composure wavered. His eyes filled with tears as he shrugged the question aside, unable to answer.

Clancy Sigal's reference to *Hollywood Babylon* was prescient. The independent film-maker Kenneth Anger, who wrote that best-selling chronicle of the seamier side of Hollywood life, soon joined the chorus of those clucking over Brando's misfortune. In a piece entitled 'Fatman in Babylon', he wrote: 'Christian Devi Brando has been a wild child all along, a druggie-alkie with a hair-trigger temper and a passion for guns since his baby days as a fought-over football in the sordid Brando/Kashfi divorce – and I do mean sordid.'

Christian Brando was 32 years old at the time of his arrest – a grown man, old enough to take responsibility for his actions without having his father called to account. But, by the harsh rules of the media, Christian was, as ever, a bit-player in his own life story. It was Marlon Brando who was really on trial – his name alone kept the story in a prominent position in newspapers and on television, even in the midst of the Gulf War with Iraq.

Kenneth Anger's style may be vulgar and excessive, but he was giving voice to the subtext of a hundred other news reports when he wrote: 'Like Jericho, the walls are down. See Marlon Brando Naked. See Marlon Brando in the Hot Seat. Woe to the Fishbowl Lifestyle of the World's Most Famous Actor. Woe to Masochist Marlon. See Him Squirm...We've had it with Zsa Zsa, we've had it with the 10-million dollar fiasco in child abuse, the McMartin Case. Time for Red Meat. Misery Time for Marlon.'

Nor were the foreign press any kinder, especially not in France where Brando had long occupied a special position of respect. Cheyenne and Dag Drollet were native Tahitians and thus French nationals. The victim's father, Jacques Drollet, used French law to accuse Cheyenne of complicity in the shooting. Characterising Christian as 'a coward, a coyote', Jacques Drollet made no secret of the fact that he held Marlon Brando responsible for his son's actions. 'He knows our Tahitian customs,' he said, 'He should have protected my son. In Tahiti the host is under an obligation to protect the guest, morally and physically.' The French press took a proprietorial interest in the case.

The respectable French daily, *Le Monde* ran a story headlined 'The Worst Role of Marlon Brando' which featured a cartoon of a scowling Brando-like figure leading a small boy by one hand and holding a revolver by its barrel in the fingers and thumb of the other hand. Blood seeps from a wound in the centre of the larger figure's chest. The implication is clear: Marlon Brando had eclipsed his son and Dag Drollet to become both the perpetrator and the victim of the killing.

A secondary reason for the murder charge being dropped (quite apart from Cheyenne's incapacity to testify) was that Christian's original statement to the police had been made before he had been properly read his rights. As a result, it was inadmissable as evidence but widely quoted in the press. 'Man, I didn't meant to shoot him,' Christian had said, 'He fought for the gun... We were rolling around on the couch...He had my hands, then *boom!* Jesus, man, it wasn't murder...Please believe me, I wouldn't do it in my father's house.'

A bail hearing for Christian Brando in May 1990 is attended by his father.

Shortly after the murder charge was dropped in favour of one of manslaughter, the popular French magazine, *Paris Match* went over the history of what it dubbed 'l'affaire Brando'. The *Match* article alleged that Marlon Brando, fearful of having his phone tapped, communicated with Cheyenne by letter and a series of personal envoys drawn from within the Brando clan, persuading her eventually to refer to the shooting as 'a tragic accident'. It explained for its readers the American legal system of 'plea-bargaining' which had allowed Christian Brando to switch from pleading 'Not Guilty' to pre-meditated murder, to plead 'Guilty' to manslaughter. At once, the maximum sentence he could receive changed from life to sixteen years' imprisonment. While Christian was facing the murder charge, *Paris Match* noted, he dressed in the negligent, long-haired style of Los Angeles' young 'marginals'; when the charge changed, Christian changed, his hair was cut short and he wore a suit and tie.

All this would be so much insinuation were it not for the final aspect of the magazine's story. Under the title, 'The Accusing Photograph', it printed a full-page colour photograph of Dag Drollet lying dead in the Brando den. With tobacco clutched in his left hand and his right index finger still pressing the keyboard of a TV remote-control switch, Drollet lies back on a couch looking, for all the world, as if he has fallen asleep in front of the television. The only evidence of foul play is the blood which stains the pillow behind him and traces along his body like a grisly red shadow. There is no sign here of the struggle that Christian had earlier maintained took place.

When Christian Brando faced the court for the last time on 26th February 1991, he received a ten-year prison sentence. Asked if Christian would appeal, the Los Angeles District Attorney replied: 'Of course

Brando tries to hold back the tears as he testifies on behalf of his son Christian during a sentencing hearing in the Santa Monica Superior Court, 28 February 1991.

not, there is nothing to appeal against.' But it was Marlon Brando who remained the focus of events. Marlon Brando who declined to swear on the Bible but agreed to swear on 'the lives of my children'; Marlon Brando who was reputedly in contact with former friends in the Black Panther movement to ensure that Christian did not have too hard a time in prison; Marlon Brando whose first choice of defence lawyer, the Civil Rights advocate William Kunstler, had been signed up by Oliver Stone to play a lawyer in his film, *The Doors*; Marlon Brando, one-time Hollywood rebel, who had finally lost his battle against the power of fantasy, of the imagined world that attaches itself to its idols, and which devours their private lives and the lives of those around them.

At 67, Marlon Brando had discovered that fame is as great an imposter as Kipling's 'Triumph and Disaster'; it did not afford him the opportunity to change the world for the better. Instead, it acted as a beacon for the malevolent moths who cluster around for some share of the light.

America still clamours for myths, and looks to Hollywood to provide them. If the western remains in eclipse, there are films like *The Godfather* saga, *Apocalypse Now* and the works of Oliver Stone to mythologise the troubles of the present century. Modern idols, too, are found in the cinema: Dean, Clift, Monroe, Welles, Brando –

Brando sits between his sons Miko (far right) and Christian on the day Christian is sentenced to ten years' imprisonment for the manslaughter of his sister's boyfriend Dag Drollet.

only these last two had the bad taste to live on beyond middle-age. Even this can be forgiven if the idol endures pain in later years. Welles lived to be 70, but died fat and neglected, looking back on a lifetime of unrealised projects. Like Welles, Brando has become an inflated parody of his younger self and Terry Malloy's speech about being a 'contender' clings as remorselessly to him as 'Over the Rainbow' did to the pathetically wasted Judy Garland. Here, indeed, is a feast for the human locusts. Yet they still feel cheated.

They feel cheated because Brando continues to mock their adulation. An intuitive actor, he has too often relied on a technique that descends into mannerism, and the early facility which was so startling at the beginning of his career has never been properly developed. Like Orson Welles, he can appear surprisingly stiff and self-conscious before the camera. These inconsistencies reveal him to be, at least from the point of view of temperament, an amateur. Brando loves acting even if he is too embarrassed to admit it, but the repetitions, delays and the sudden urgent calls on stamina which are essential parts of the job hold no appeal for him.

His concentration span now extends only as far as the next cue card but in the days when he could maintain his interest and commitment he provided a clutch of performances which are among the most effective ever recorded on film. He gave the impression that the emotions he portrayed were real – felt and not manufactured.

David Lean's film of *Nostromo* offered Brando an extraordinary role as the malevolent Minister of War, but the actor had dropped out of the cast long before the project was finally halted by Lean's death in April, 1991. Meanwhile, Andrew Bergman is still hoping to sign Brando for *The Freshman II* and Harold Evans has purchased the unwritten autobiography for Random House. One of Brando's last abiding dreams, an epic film which treats the Native American with dignity, has been realised by Kevin Costner in *Dances with Wolves* which opened to critical acclaim and was rewarded with a clutch of Oscars. There will be more offers, other projects. But, for the moment, Brando may prefer to be remembered for his considerable work with the American Indian Movement – and there are many who will long cherish him for that – and for his Civil Rights work. He must certainly be concerned about the future of his extended family. He has often remarked that he is a reflective man – he has much to reflect upon.

His private life has been subsumed into the legend. Even as a fat old man with little remaining of the beauty which was once the only thing that his friends and enemies could agree upon, he is not allowed his ordinariness. Marlon Brando cannot be ordinary because he carries the burden of dreams we have invested in him. He has entered the collective consciousness as Stanley Kowalski, Terry Malloy, Johnny of *The Wild One* and the pathetic Paul of *Last Tango in Paris*. The consensus view is that Brando has lived his life on film.

If he mocks his admirers, it matters little; they will go on holding fast to their illusion. The Brando legend has finally obliterated the truth, and the achievements of his professional life count for little. The influence remains, of course, for other actors. Robert de Niro's portrayal of Jake Le Motta quoting Terry Malloy's 'contender' speech has become an even more poignant *hommage* given the emotional battering Brando has received in recent years. At the same time, one of the pleasures of Coppola's youth movie, *Rumble Fish* is an unintentionally comic scene in which Mickey Rourke and Matt Dillon try to 'out-Brando' each other, their mannered posing reminding you of just how good the original article really was. But what matters for most of Brando's followers is that he ignited the sexual imaginations of people who had no desire to confront the humanity of the real man. As he himself once said: 'I'm just another sonofabitch sitting in a motor home on a film set, and they come looking for Zeus.'

When Marlon Brando himself is nothing more than a memory, the necromantic young who attach themselves now to the shades of Monroe, Dean and Clift, will again come looking for Zeus. Just occasionally, when watching Brando's image on the screen, they may believe they have found him. The rest is show business.

189

FILMOGRAPHY

THE MEN (1950)
UNITED ARTISTS
Directed by Fred Zinnemann
Produced by Stanley Kramer
Screenplay by Carl Foreman
Music by Dimitri Tiomkin
Cinematographer: Robert de Grasse
Running time: 85 mins
Main cast: Marlon Brando (Ken Wilocek), Teresa Wright, Everett Sloane, Jack Webb, Howard St John

A STREETCAR NAMED DESIRE (1951)
WARNER BROS
Directed by Elia Kazan
Produced by Charles K Feldman
Screenplay by Tennessee Williams
Music by Alex North
Cinematographer: Harry Stradling
Running time: 122 mins
Main cast: Marlon Brando (Stanley Kowalski), Vivien Leigh, Kim Hunter, Karl Malden

VIVA ZAPATA! (1952)
20th CENTURY-FOX
Directed by Elia Kazan
Produced by Darryl F Zanuck
Screenplay by John Steinbeck
Music by Alex North
Cinematographer: Joe MacDonald
Running time: 113 mins
Main cast: Marlon Brando (Emiliano Zapata), Jean Peters, Joseph Wiseman, Anthony Quinn

JULIUS CAESAR (1953) MGM
Directed by Joseph L Mankiewicz
Produced by John Houseman
Screenplay by Joseph L Mankiewicz
Music by Miklos Rozsa
Cinematographer: Joseph Ruttenberg
Running time: 121 mins
Main cast: Marlon Brando (Mark Antony), John Gielgud, James Mason, Greer Garson, Deborah Kerr, Louis Calhern, Edmond O'Brien, George Macready, Michael Pate, John Hoyt, Alan Napier

THE WILD ONE (1953)
COLUMBIA
Directed by Laslo Benedek
Produced by Stanley Kramer
Screenplay by John Paxton
Music by Leith Stevens
Cinematographer: Hal Mohr
Running time: 79 mins
Main cast: Marlon Brando (Johnny), Lee Marvin, Mary

Murphy, Robert Keith, Jay C Flippen

ON THE WATERFRONT (1954) COLUMBIA
Directed by Elia Kazan
Produced by Sam Spiegel
Screenplay by Budd Schulberg
Music by Leonard Bernstein
Cinematographer: Boris Kaufman
Running time: 108 mins
Main cast: Marlon Brando (Terry Malloy), Eva Marie Saint, Lee J Cobb, Rod Steiger, Karl Malden, Pat Henning, Leif Erickson, James Westerfield, John Hamilton

DESIRÉE (1954)
20th CENTURY-FOX
Directed by Henry Koster
Produced by Julius Blaustein
Screenplay by Daniel Taradash
Music by Alex North
Cinematographer: Milton Krasner
Running time: 110 mins
Main cast: Marlon Brando (Napoleon Bonaparte), Jean Simmons, Merle Oberon, Michael Rennie

GUYS AND DOLLS (1955)
MGM
Directed by Joseph L Mankiewicz
Produced by Samuel Goldwyn
Screenplay by Joseph L Mankiewicz
Music and lyrics by Frank Loesser
Cinematographer: Harry Stradling
Running time: 149 mins
Main cast: Marlon Brando (Sky Masterson), Frank Sinatra, Jean Simmons, Vivian Blaine, Stubby Kaye, B S Pully, Robert Keith, Sheldon Leonard, George E Stone

THE TEAHOUSE OF THE AUGUST MOON (1956) MGM
Directed by Daniel Mann
Produced by Jack Cummings
Screenplay by John Patrick
Music by Saul Chaplin
Cinematographer: John Alton
Running time: 123 mins
Main cast: Marlon Brando (Sakini), Glenn Ford, Eddie Albert, Paul Ford, Machiko Kyo, Henry Morgan

SAYONARA (1957)
GOETZ-PENNEBAKER-WARNER BROS
Directed by Joshua Logan
Produced by William Goetz
Screenplay by Paul Osborn
Music by Franz Waxman
Cinematographer: Ellsworth Fredericks
Running time: 147 mins

Main cast: Marlon Brando (Major Lloyd Gruver), Miyoshi Umeki, Miiko Taka, Red Buttons, Ricardo Montalban, Patricia Owens, Kent Smith, Martha Scott, James Garner

THE YOUNG LIONS (1958)
20th CENTURY-FOX
Directed by Edward Dmytryk
Produced by Al Lichtman
Screenplay by Edward Anhalt
Music by Hugo Friedhofer
Cinematographer: Joe MacDonald
Running time: 167 mins
Main cast: Marlon Brando (Christian Diestl), Montgomery Clift, Dean Martin, Hope Lange, Barbara Rush, May Britt, Maximilian Schell, Lee Van Cleef

THE FUGITIVE KIND (1960)
PENNEBAKER-UNITED ARTISTS
Directed by Sidney Lumet
Produced by Martin Jurow, Richard A Shepherd
Screenplay by Tennessee Williams and Meade Roberts
Music by Kenyon Hopkins
Cinematographer: Boris Kaufman
Running time: 119 mins
Main cast: Marlon Brando (Val Xavier), Anna Magnani, Victor Jory, Joanne Woodward, Maureen Stapleton

ONE-EYED JACKS (1961)
PENNEBAKER-PARAMOUNT
Directed by Marlon Brando
Produced by Frank P Rosenberg
Screenplay by Guy Trooper and Calder Willingham
Music by Hugo Friedhofer
Cinematographer: Charles Lang
Running time: 141 mins
Main cast: Marlon Brando (Rio), Karl Malden, Pina Pellicer, Katy Jurado, Slim Pickens, Ben Johnson, Timothy Carey, Elisha Cook Jnr

MUTINY ON THE BOUNTY (1962) MGM
Directed by Lewis Milestone
Produced by Aaron Rosenberg
Screenplay by Charles Lederer
Music by Bronislau Kaper
Cinematographer: Robert Surtees
Running time: 185 mins
Main cast: Marlon Brando (Fletcher Christian), Trevor Howard, Richard Harris, Hugh Griffith, Tarita, Richard Haydn, Percy Herbert, Duncan Lamont, Gordon Jackson, Chips Rafferty, Noel Purcell

THE UGLY AMERICAN (1963) UNIVERSAL
Directed by George Englund

Produced by George Englund
Screenplay by Stewart Stern
Music by Frank Skinner
Cinematographer: Clifford Stine
Running time: 120 mins
Main cast: Marlon Brando (Harrison Carter MacWhite), Eiji Okada, Sandra Church, Pat Hingle, Arthur Hill, Jocelyn Brando, Kukrit Pramoj

BEDTIME STORY (1964)
PENNEBAKER-UNIVERSAL
Directed by Ralph Levy
Produced by Stanley Shapiro
Screenplay by Stanley Shapiro and Paul Henning
Music by Hans J Salter
Cinematographer: Clifford Stine
Running time: 99 mins
Main cast: Marlon Brando (Fred Benson), David Niven, Shirley Jones, Dody Goodman, Aram Stephen, Marie Windsor

MORITURI (1965)
(UK TITLE: THE SABOTEUR, CODE NAME MORITURI)
20th CENTURY-FOX
Directed by Bernhard Wicki
Produced by Aaron Rosenberg
Screenplay by Daniel Taradash
Music by Jerry Goldsmith
Cinematographer: Conrad Hall
Running time: 122 mins
Main cast: Marlon Brando (Robert Crain), Yul Brynner, Trevor Howard, Janet Margolin, Wally Cox

THE CHASE (1966)
COLUMBIA
Directed by Arthur Penn
Produced by Sam Spiegel
Screenplay by Lillian Hellman
Music by John Barry
Cinematographer: Joseph La Shelle
Running time: 135 mins
Main cast: Marlon Brando (Sheriff Calder), Jane Fonda, Robert Redford, Angie Dickinson, Janice Rule, James Fox, Robert Duvall, E G Marshall, Miriam Hopkins

THE APPALOOSA
(UK TITLE: SOUTHWEST TO SONORA) (1966) UNIVERSAL
Directed by Sidney J Furie
Produced by Alan Miller
Screenplay by James Bridges and Roland Kibbee
Music by Frank Skinner
Cinematographer: Russell Metty
Running time: 99 mins
Main cast: Marlon Brando (Matt), Anjanette Comer, John Saxon, Rafael Campos

A COUNTESS FROM HONG KONG (1967) UNIVERSAL
Directed by Charles Chaplin

Produced by Jerome Epstein
Screenplay by Charles Chaplin
Music by Charles Chaplin
Cinematographer: Arthur Ibbetson
Running time: 120 mins
Main cast: Marlon Brando (Ogden Mears), Sophia Loren, Patrick Cargill, Margaret Rutherford, Charles Chaplin, Sydney Chaplin, Oliver Johnston, John Paul

REFLECTIONS IN A GOLDEN EYE (1967)
WARNER BROS
Directed by John Huston
Produced by Ray Stark
Screenplay by Chapman Mortimer and Gladys Hill
Music by Toshiro Mayuzumi
Cinematographer: Aldo Tonti
Running time: 108 mins
Main cast: Marlon Brando (Major Weldon Penderton), Elizabeth Taylor, Brian Keith, Julie Harris, Robert Forster

CANDY (1968) CINERAMA
Directed by Christian Marquand
Produced by Robert Haggiag
Screenplay by Buck Henry
Music by Dave Grusin
Cinematographer: Giuseppe Rotunno
Running time: 124 mins
Main cast: Marlon Brando (Grindl), Ewa Aulin, Richard Burton, James Coburn, Walter Matthau, Charles Aznavour, John Huston, Elsa Martinelli, Ringo Starr, John Astin

THE NIGHT OF THE FOLLOWING DAY (1969)
UNIVERSAL
Directed by Hubert Cornfield
Produced by Hubert Cornfield
Screenplay by Hubert Cornfield and Robert Phippeny
Music by Stanley Myers
Cinematographer: Willy Kurant
Running time: 100 mins
Main cast: Marlon Brando (Bud), Richard Boone, Rita Moreno, Pamela Franklin

QUEIMADA! (US TITLE: BURN!) (1970)
UNITED ARTISTS
Directed by Gillo Pontecorvo
Produced by Alberto Grimaldi
Screenplay by Franco Solinas and Giorgio Arlorio
Music by Ennio Morricone
Cinematographer: Marcello Gatti
Running time: 132 mins
Main cast: Marlon Brando (Sir William Walker), Renato Salvatori, Norman Hill

THE NIGHTCOMERS (1971)
AVCO EMBASSY

Directed by Michael Winner
Produced by Michael Winner
Screenplay by Michael Hastings
Music by Jerry Fielding
Cinematographer: Robert Paynter
Running time: 96 mins
Main cast: Marlon Brando (Peter Quint), Stephanie Beacham, Thora Hird, Harry Andrews, Verna Harvey, Christopher Ellis, Anna Palk

THE GODFATHER (1972)
PARAMOUNT
Directed by Francis Ford Coppola
Produced by Albert S Ruddy
Screenplay by Francis Ford Coppola and Mario Puzo
Music by Nino Rota
Cinematographer: Gordon Willis
Running time: 175 mins
Main cast: Marlon Brando (Don Vito Corleone), Al Pacino, Robert Duvall, James Caan, Richard Castellano, Diane Keaton, Talia Shire, Richard Conte, John Marley, Sterling Hayden, John Cazale

LAST TANGO IN PARIS (1972) UNITED ARTISTS
Directed by Bernardo Bertolucci
Produced by Alberto Grimaldi
Screenplay by Bernardo Bertolucci and Franco Arcalli
Music by Gato Barbieri
Cinematographer: Vittorio Storaro
Running time: 129 mins
Main cast: Marlon Brando (Paul), Maria Schneider, Jean-Pierre Leaud, Catherine Allegret, Maria Michi

THE MISSOURI BREAKS (1976) UNITED ARTISTS
Directed by Arthur Penn
Produced by Robert M Sherman
Screenplay by Thomas McGuane
Music by John Williams
Cinematographer: Michael Butler
Running time: 126 mins
Main cast: Marlon Brando (Robert Lee Clayton), Jack Nicholson, Randy Quaid, Kathleen Lloyd, Frederic Forrest, Harry Dean Stanton, John McLian, John P Ryan, Richard Bradford

SUPERMAN (1978)
WARNER BROS
Directed by Richard Donner
Produced by Pierre Spengler
Screenplay by Mario Puzo, David Newman, Robert Benton and Leslie Newman
Music by John Williams
Cinematographer: Geoffrey

Unsworth
Running time: 142 mins
Main cast: Marlon Brando (Jor-El), Christopher Reeve, Margot Kidder, Jackie Cooper, Glenn Ford, Phyllis Thaxter, Trevor Howard, Gene Hackman, Ned Beatty, Susannah York

APOCALYPSE NOW (1979)
UNITED ARTISTS
Directed by Francis Ford Coppola
Produced by Francis Ford Coppola
Screenplay by John Milius and Francis Ford Coppola
Music by Carmine Coppola, Francis Ford Coppola
Cinematographer: Vittoria Storaro
Running time: 153 mins
Main cast: Marlon Brando (Colonel Walter Kurtz), Martin Sheen, Robert Duvall, Frederic Forrest, Sam Bottoms, Dennis Hopper, Harrison Ford, Albert Hall, Larry Fishburne, Scott Glenn

THE FORMULA (1980) MGM
Directed by John G Avildsen
Produced by Steve Shagan
Screenplay by Steve Shagan
Music by Bill Conti
Cinematographer: James Crabe
Running time: 117 mins
Main cast: Marlon Brando (Adam Steiffel), George C Scott, Marthe Keller, John Gielgud, Beatrice Straight, Richard Lynch

A DRY WHITE SEASON (1989) MGM
Directed by Euzhan Palcy
Produced by Paula Weinstein
Screenplay by Colin Welland and Euzhan Palcy
Music by Dave Grusin
Cinematographer: Kevin Pike and Pierre-William Glenn
Running time: 107 mins
Main cast: Marlon Brando (Ian McKenzie), Donald Sutherland, Janet Suzman, Zakes Mokae, Jurgen Prochnow, Susan Sarandon, Winston Ntshona, Thoko Ntshinga

THE FRESHMAN (1990)
TRI-STAR
Directed by Andrew Bergman
Produced by Mike Lobell
Screenplay by Andrew Bergman
Music by David Newman
Cinematographer: William A Fraker
Running time: 102 mins
Main cast: Marlon Brando (Carmine Sabatini), Matthew Broderick, Bruno Kirby, Penelope Ann Miller, Frank Whaley, Jon Polito, Paul Benedict, Maximilian Schell

THEATRE CREDITS

I REMEMBER MAMA (1944)
Playwright: John Van Druten
Director: John Van Druten
Main cast: Marlon Brando, Joan Tetzel, Mady Christians, Richard Bishop, Carolyn Hummel, Frances Heflin, Oswald Marshall

TRUCKLINE CAFE (1946)
Playwright: Maxwell Anderson
Director: Harold Clurman
Main cast: Marlon Brando, Frank Overton, Ralph Theadore, John Sweet, Kevin McCarthy, June Walker, Karl Malden, Ann Shepherd

CANDIDA (1946)
Playwright: George Bernard Shaw
Director: Guthrie McClintic
Main cast: Marlon Brando, Mildred Natwick, Wesley Addy, Olivier Cliff, Cedric Hardwicke, Katharine Cornell

A FLAG IS BORN (1946)
Playwright: Ben Hecht
Director: Luther Adler
Main cast: Marlon Brando, Quentin Reynolds, Paul Muni, Celia Adler, Mario Berini, George David Baxter

THE EAGLE HAS TWO HEADS (1946)
Playwright: Jean Cocteau
Main cast: Marlon Brando (first night only), Tallulah Bankhead

A STREETCAR NAMED DESIRE (1947)
Playwright: Tennessee Williams
Director: Elia Kazan
Main cast: Marlon Brando, Jessica Tandy, Kim Hunter, Karl Malden

ARMS AND THE MAN (1953)
Playwright: George Bernard Shaw
Main cast: Marlon Brando, William Redfield, Carlo Fiore

TELEVISION CREDITS

ROOTS: THE NEXT GENERATIONS (1979) ABC
Directed by John Erman, Charles S Dubin, George Stanford Brown and Lloyd Richards
Produced by David Wolper
Cinematographer: Joseph M Wilcots
Running time: 6 x 96 mins
Main cast: Marlon Brando (George Lincoln Rockwell), James Earl Jones, George Stanford, Olivia de Havilland, Henry Fonda, Greg Morris

Acknowledgements

For their assistance in supplying valuable material and comments, I am grateful to Sally Belfrage, Douglas K Dempsey, Dominique Lebrun, Marcus Lee, Nasreen Memon (NFT), Susan Fantini (NFT), David Thompson (BBC TV), Karen Thorson, Lucy Vinson (Columbia Tri-Star) and special thanks to Chris Rodley and Juliette Greco.

The task of research has been made easier by the large number of books which chart or make reference to Brando's career and I am indebted to the authors and publishers of the following: *Marlon Brando* by David Shipman; *Marlon Brando* by René Jordan; *Brando: The Unauthorised Biography* by Charles Higham; *Brando* by Bob Thomas; *Marlon Brando* by David Downing; *The Films of Marlon Brando* by Tony Thomas; *Bud: The Brando I Knew* by Carlo Fiore; *Brando For Breakfast* by Anna Kashfi and E P Stein; *Brando* by Charles Hamblett; *Brando In The Camera Eye* by Sam Shaw; *Marlon Brando* by Alan Frank; *Elia Kazan: An American Odyssey* edited by Michel Ciment; *A Life* by Elia Kazan; *Timebends* by Arthur Miller; *Front and Centre* by John Houseman; *An Actor and His Time* by John Gielgud; *Pictures Will Talk: The Life and Films of Joseph L Mankiewicz* by Kenneth L Geist; *Trevor Howard, A Gentleman and A Player* by Vivienne Knight; *Letters From An Actor* by William Redfield; *An Open Book* by John Huston; *A Private View* by Irene Mayer Selznick; *The Playboy Interview* edited by Barry G Colson; *Memoirs* by Tennessee Williams; *The Kindness of Strangers* by Donald Spoto; *Scratch An Actor* by Sheilah Graham; *It's Only A Movie, Ingrid* by Alexander Walker; *Montgomery Clift* by Patricia Bosworth; *Monty* by Robert LaGuardia; *In Search of Theatre* by Eric Bentley; *Billy Wilder in Hollywood* by Maurice Zolotow; *Nostalgia Isn't What It Used To Be* by Simone Signoret. In addition, the latter stages of this book were helped by the existence of some fine journalism, particularly by the aforementioned Chris Rodley and by Clancy Sigal.

I would also like to thank the following individuals, picture agencies, newspapers and magazines who contributed to the gathering of photographs and visual material for the book: Aquarius Picture Library; Associated Press; Robin Bean; British Film Institute; Camera Press; Cecil Beaton Archive/Sotheby's; Christophe L. Collection; Fans Star Library; Film Review magazine; Gamma Presse Images; Hulton-Deutsch Collection; Mander and Mitchenson Collection; Nadia McLeod for loaning material from her collection; Museum of the City of New York; National Film Archive; New York Public Library/Theatre Collection; New York Public Library/Vandamm Collection; Picture Post; Edward Quinn.

A very special thanks to Robin Bean for his efficient and enthusiastic help in providing invaluable photographs from his collection.

Several friends have eased the writing process, among them Amanda Boxer, Carolyn Courage, Karen Elliott, Joanna Foster, Tony Meyer, Pravin, Nitin, Gita and Bena Patel, Eve Pomerance, Malcolm, Anne, Ellen and Katy Taylor and Helen Teague. Thanks also to the BFI Stills Library for their help and courtesy. Sandra Wake and Terry Porter of Plexus have been models of support and encouragement, as has my editor Nicky Adamson who, together with Annette McFadyen and Claire Grainger coaxed and cajoled the book into shape.

Finally, my warm thanks to Lindsay Anderson whose support never waivered and who was often a firm Brittles to my errant Quincannon and to Catherine Gray, whose encouragement is only part of the story.